WALK, DON'T DIE

How to Stay Fit, Trim and Healthy Without Killing Yourself

OTHER BOOKS BY THE AUTHOR:

WALK, DON'T RUN. Philadelphia: Medical Manor Press, 1979.

THE DOCTOR'S WALKING BOOK. New York: Ballantine Books, *1980*.

THE DOCTOR'S WALKING DIET. Philadelphia: Medical Manor Books®, 1982.

DIETWALK®: THE DOCTOR'S FAST 3-DAY SUPERDIET. Philadelphia: Medical Manor Books®, 1983.

WALK, DON'T RUN II. Philadelphia: Medical Manor Books®, 1986.

Medical Manor Books® are available at special quantity discounts for bulk purchases for sales promotions, premiums, fund raising or educational use. Book excerpts can also be created to fit specific needs.

For details write the Special Markets Dept. of Medical Manor Books®, 3501 Newberry Road, Philadelphia, PA 19154.

WALK, DON'T DIE

How to Stay Fit, Trim and Healthy Without Killing Yourself

By
Fred A. Stutman, M.D.

MEDICAL MANOR BOOKS®
Philadelphia, PA

WALK, DON'T DIE

How to Stay Fit, Trim and Healthy
Without Killing Yourself

MEDICAL MANOR BOOKS® is the registered trademark of Manor House Publications, Inc. REG. U.S. PAT. OFF.

DIETSTEP® is the registered trademark of Dr. Stutman's Walking-Off-Weight Program. REG. U.S. PAT. OFF.

TRIMSTEP™ is the trademark of Dr. Stutman's Body-Shaping Walking Program.

FIT-STEP™ is the trademark of Dr. Stutman's Fitness Walking Program.

Library of Congress Catalog Card Number 85-06336
ISBN 0-934232-05-9—paper
ISBN 0-934232-06-7—cloth

First Edition: November 1986
Manufactured in the United States of America

To
Suzanne
Craig, Rhonda, Robert
Irene and George

And to

*The millions of Americans who have been
brain-washed by joggers and so-called
fitness experts into believing the fallacy that
exercise has to be painful or stressful in order
to be beneficial*

Also to

*Gerry, whose party I inadvertently missed,
while I was working on this manuscript*

AUTHOR'S CAUTION

"EVEN THOUGH WALKING IS ONE OF THE SAFEST AND LEAST STRENUOUS FORMS OF EXERCISE, IT IS STILL ESSENTIAL THAT YOU CONSULT YOUR OWN PHYSICIAN BEFORE BEGINNING THIS WALKING EXERCISE PROGRAM."

Fred A. Stutman, M.D.

ACKNOWLEDGEMENTS

EDITOR: Dr. Suzanne T. Stutman

MANAGING EDITOR: Patricia McGarvey

ASSOCIATE EDITOR: Carol A. Verdi, M.D.

ASSISTANT EDITOR: Maryanne Johnston

EDITORIAL STAFF: Sheryl Bartkus, Ann Birchler, Rose Schmidt, Linda Quinn

MEDICAL CHARTS & ILLUSTRATIONS: Medical Times, a Romaine Pierson Publication; Medical Tribune, Inc.; The Physician and Sportsmedicine, a McGraw-Hill Publication; Stuart Pharmaceuticals, Div. of ICI Americas, Inc.; U.S.V. Laboratories, Inc.; Washington Post Writers Group

PRODUCT PERMISSION: The Body Shoe® by Hush Puppies® Shoes—Wolverine World Wide, Inc.; Butter Buds®, Butter Buds Div., Cumberland Packing Corp.; Egg Beaters®, Fleischmann, Div., Nabisco Brands Inc.; Superpretzel®, J & J Snack Foods, Inc.

CARTOONS: Berke Breathed, Reg Hider, Norm Rockwell

WORD PROCESSING: Hadassah Freifelder: The Automated Typist, Philadelphia, PA

TYPOGRAPHY: Graphic Arts Composition, Philadelphia, PA

BOOK PRODUCTION: The Maple-Vail Book Manufacturing Group, York, PA

PUBLISHER: Medical Manor Books®, Philadelphia, PA

"I TOLD YOU SO, HARRIET. THERE'S NOT EVEN ONE 'WALKER' BURIED HERE!"

TABLE OF CONTENTS

"I have met with but one or two persons in the course of my life who understood the art of walking. Every journey begins with the first step and every walk is a sort of crusade."

—Henry David Thoreau

INTRODUCTION

"Every Journey Begins With The First Step"

Seven years have elapsed since the publication of my first book entitled, **WALK, DON'T RUN**. During that time thousands of joggers have died needlessly and literally millions of joggers have sustained serious injuries. The statistics of death by jogging have steadily increased over the past 10 years since the dawn of jogger-mania. Only recently, after several well known athletes and sportsmen died from this barbaric form of self-punishment, has the American public begun to realize the very real dangers of jogging—"He was awfully young, wasn't he?" or "I thought joggers had strong hearts!"

As early as 1979 the Journal of the American Medical Association published an article entitled, "Death During Jogging or Running: A Study of 18 Cases." This article, cited in my 1979 edition of **WALK, DONT RUN**, received considerable criticism at the time. It was said that these were isolated cases and unlikely to occur with any regularity. Well, unfortunately, this was not the case as the families of many dead joggers were soon to realize. Don't tell these wives about statistics; their husbands are 100 percent dead.

Deaths from jogging and jogging-related injuries have occurred with such frequency and regularity over the past decade that I contend that The Food and Drug Administration should require jogging shoes, like cigarettes, to carry a warning label **"CAUTION— JOGGING CAN BE HAZARDOUS TO YOUR HEALTH—PROCEED AT YOUR OWN RISK."** I truly feel that this danger cannot be dismissed too lightly, since the medical evidence is now strongly against jogging and in favor of more moderate exercises like walking.

Why tempt fate? With all the hazards and dangers of jogging there is now no reason whatsoever that exercise has to be painful or stressful to be beneficial. On the contrary, all the fitness, weight control, health and medical benefits are obtained by walking at 1/1000 the risk. And what's more, it's fun, it doesn't hurt and you can walk for a lifetime. Longevity equals walking and walking equals longevity. Let's live long enough to have fun, so **Walk, Don't Run**.

And now with the addition of fitness clubs, aerobics classes, exercise clinics and weight-machines, we are faced with new injuries, disabilities and in some cases even death. These so-called fitness-builders are no more than glorified calisthenics, each with its own specific hazards and dangers. Not only are you unduly stressing your cardiovascular and muscular systems but you are straining your wallets to pay for these elusive fitness benefits. And the basic unalterable truth again is that you get the same health, fitness, and weight control benefits with walking without the added risk of disease, disability, and death. It's easy to be fit so don't pout, just **Walk, Don't Workout!**

Inactivity on the other hand, is just as bad for you as strenuous exercise or jogging. More and more studies have shown the increased incidence of hypertension, heart disease, diabetes, vascular disease, obesity and premature aging in the inactive person. Even cancer of the colon has a higher incidence in the sedentary individual. So if you want to live a long life and stay fit, then **Walk, Don't Sit!**

Weight-loss centers, diet drugs, special protein mixes, fast weight-loss plans and the latest fad diet programs are nothing but plain old-fashioned diet gimmicks. They promise you everlasting weight-loss; however, the only thing that gets permanently thin is your bankroll. Each plan claims quick weight-loss results. What they don't tell you is that the weight gain after the initial weight loss is even quicker. Not only do you end up fatter in the gut and thinner in the wallet after the diet gimmick runs its course, but you actually risk life and limb in the process. Fad and gimmick diet plans have one thing in common—they are dangerous. And they can cause disease, disability and even death. Walking will keep you thin if you try it, just **Walk, Don't Diet!**

This book was primarily written for my patients who have spent a lifetime on diet and fitness programs and were frustrated by their poor results, and who incidentally endangered their lives in the process. After many years of research I have developed the first medically formulated lifetime weight-control and exercise program for permanent weight loss, physical fitness and longevity. This program was designed with your life in mind. You can be sure of one thing—you won't die walking!

Walking is the road to good health, physical fitness and a thin, trim figure. There is no need to resort to death-defying diets, back-breaking calisthenics or dangerous heart-pounding exercises in order to be fit and trim. You can now lose weight and exercise safely without the dangers of disease, disability and death. And I guarantee you that if you take these "steps" you'll delay your death. So **Walk, Don't Die**, it's certainly worth a try. What do you have to lose—only your life!

"THE FIRST-AID STATION IS RIGHT DOWN THE ROAD, FOLKS!"

I. WALK, DON'T RUN

"It is unfortunate that it took the tragic death of the famous author and runner Jim Fixx to get people thinking that running may not be the best form of aerobic exercise."

Fred A. Stutman, M.D.
Shape Magazine, March 1986

"THAT'S WHAT I CALL REALLY RUNNING YOURSELF INTO THE GROUND!"

CHAPTER 1

DEAD JOGGERS TELL NO TALES

THE FIRST NAIL IN THE COFFIN

In my first book, entitled **Walk, Don't Run**, I reviewed a study published in the Journal of the American Medical Association entitled **"Death During Jogging or Running: A Study of 18 Cases"**— 9/21/79. At that time jogging was reaching its peak as the number one crazy fad exercise in America. No one at that time was about to pay any notice to a so-called isolated study of only 18 deaths.

Many of the thousands of dead joggers might still be alive today had they paid attention to this study which appropriately began **"Neither superior physical fitness nor habitual physical activity guarantees against an exercise death."** Of these 18 runners, all but two had trained regularly for years. Only one person was known to have had a previous history of heart disease.

Autopsies revealed that 13 out of 18 of these deaths were caused by coronary heart disease—in these apparently normal healthy runners who thought they were free of heart disease. One death was caused by an inflammation of the heart muscle, another death resulted from heat stroke, and no clear-cut diagnosis could be determined in the remaining three dead joggers.

However, recent studies have shown that in deaths from jogging, where no cause can be found at autopsy, death actually resulted from a sudden *spasm of the coronary arteries*, caused by the extreme stress of jogging. This spasm of the artery causes a lack of blood supply to the heart, often resulting in a *fatal arrhythmia* (a wild uncontrolled erratic heartbeat) which results in *cardiac arrest*. At autopsy, however, everything looks squeaky clean: no artery spasm noted and no apparent heart damage present, because the blood supply wasn't cut off long enough to cause any dead tissue in the heart—just long enough to cause the fatal irregular heartbeat and sudden death. The autopsy diagnosis: **an apparently normal heart and coronary arteries in another dead jogger!**

In most cases, however, death from jogging results from underlying, undiagnosed coronary heart disease. The autopsy findings then will usually reveal blocked arteries, which result in the death of the heart muscle from a lack of blood supply. Well then, why were these nuts running in the first place? Because another nut probably told them that running prevents heart disease. In the 70's there was a myth circulating that no marathon runner ever died of heart disease. This eventually took a lot of explaining to the wives of many dead runners who died of cardiac arrest during their races.

This little-known article ended with the appropriate warning: *"More data on the risk-benefit ratio of endurance exercise is needed."* Over the past 7 years since this report was published, more than enough medical data has been studied to show that the risk of disease, disability and death from jogging and other strenuous sports far outweighs any minimal benefits that you could get from these dangerous exercises.

Walk, Don't Run, and you'll exercise for fun. If you run, it's like playing with a loaded gun!

THE JOGGING MYTH

The National Institutes of Health recently reported on a stŭdy of runners who were apparently free of any heart disease but who died while jogging. Autopsies revealed that they all had coronary arteries that were clogged with cholesterol deposits which led to their deaths. In these particular runners, jogging didn't prolong their lives, it actually hastened their deaths. These individuals all had blood cholesterol levels over 230 mg.

This study points out two particularly interesting facts. One, that high levels of cholesterol lead to premature coronary artery disease. And secondly, that jogging does not prevent heart disease, but may actually precipitate a fatal heart attack in people with narrowed arteries from too much cholesterol. These people would have died sooner or later because of the cholesterol deposits; however, jogging made it that much sooner because of the added stress on the coronaries. And what's more, many of these people might have sought medical help earlier in their disease process, if they had not erroneously thought that jogging was "all the medicine they needed." This long-time myth that jogging prevents heart disease must finally be *laid to rest* with the rest of the dead joggers.

ON YOUR MARK, GET SET, YOU'RE DEAD!

According to recent conclusive medical research, vigorous exercise like jogging creates a temporary hypertension or high blood pressure in the arteries. Small breaks form in the walls of the arteries causing a tiny amount of bleeding. These breaks are repaired by the body's healing processes. However, this break or crack in the artery wall forms a type of scar. This scar tissue then becomes the site for deposits of cholesterol and calcium, leading eventually to a narrowing of the artery at this injured site.

With repeated bouts of vigorous exercise come repeated small tears or breaks in the artery walls. These additional tears usually heal also; however, each tear attracts deposits of cholesterol and calcium to further narrow the artery's lumen (opening). This may eventually lead to a complete blockage of the artery, with the end result of either a stroke or a heart attack.

Hypertension or high blood pressure starts to develop when the jogger's pulse rate reaches 120 beats per minute. At a pulse rate of 140 or above, approximately 95 percent of people are in a high blood pressure or hypertensive condition. Is that good? Certainly not! It's downright dangerous! So what's all this talk about exercise being good for you only if your pulse rate goes above 140 beats per minute? It's the biggest hoax that has been perpetrated on the American public since the Orson Welles radio news-broadcast about a Martian invasion on earth in the late 1930's.

There has never been any medical validation to the high pulse-rate fitness theory. No one has ever proven that the faster your heart goes the more fit you are. No scientific, physiological or medical proof exists anywhere in the world that racing your heart like a maniac actually strengthens your heart. On the contrary, a rapid heart rate sustained for long periods of time can be potentially dangerous, not beneficial. And in fact more valid medical studies are appearing with increased frequency, showing that the average American is at danger of developing premature heart disease, stroke and sudden death from strenuous exercise.

On your mark, get set—you're dead!

Walk, Don't Run! There's many a dead jogger along the race courses of America. Don't you be one of life's unnecessary casualties. If you want to stay alive, *Walk, Don't Die!*

HAVE YOU EVER SEEN
A JOGGER SMILE?

Walking remains the safest, most effective form of exercise known to man. With all of the hazards of jogging and competitive sports you may wonder why anyone would participate in so violent an exercise as jogging. Well, the answer is simple—we live in a masochistic society and we have been conditioned to believe that an exercise or activity has to be painful in order for it to be beneficial. For instance, how many of you have attempted to diet with vigorous starvation diets to obtain a thin figure, engaged in back-breaking exercises to have a well-conditioned trim body, or suffered a painful sunburn to obtain a beautiful tan. *Have you ever seen a jogger smile?* They can't; it hurts too much.

Medical research has proven that exercise does not have to be painful in order to have beneficial results. Walking produces the same—let me repeat—the same health, fitness and weight control benefits as jogging and other strenuous exercises without the hazards. The cardiovascular benefits are exactly the same without the strain.

These are not only my own observations, but are the conclusions of thousands of medical investigators in this country and abroad. The medical journals are filled with studies about the health benefits of walking, and they are also filled with an equal number of reports listing the hazards of jogging and other strenuous exercises. So, don't be dumb; let's have some fun— *Walk, Don't Run!*

Remember, you can achieve better health and fitness without stress and strain and inconvenience—and let me point out to you that a walking program is the

only exercise that you can safely carry out for the rest
of your life. Walking, then, is the road to a healthier,
happier, and longer life.

TIME-BOMBS
EXPLODE ON IMPACT

Millions of Americans have serious heart disease
and have no symptoms whatsoever. They work, they
play, they have fun and their first symptom of heart
trouble may be sudden death.

Your arteries don't close up overnight. It's a gradual process and they may take years of abuse before
they narrow down completely. Many people are walking around symptom-free with one, two, and in many
cases, three blocked coronary arteries leading to their
hearts. Remember, I said **walking around**! These so-
called walking time-bombs usually won't go off without
some warning signs, like chest pain, unless the walking time-bomb is dumb enough to become a running
time-bomb. Then they **explode on impact** and they're
labeled another "jogging death." "He wasn't sick a day
in his life; he never had a pain or an ache," and so on
and so forth.

The statistics indicate that the incidence of sudden death in runners is 9-10 times that of non-runners.
But the runners say that only one or two in 10,000
runners die every year from running. I say, those statistics stink! Out of 30 or more million runners, that's
an awful lot of unnecessary deaths every year. And
remember that the one or two out of every 10,000
runners that die are 100 percent dead! **Walk, Don't
Die**, don't leave your family high and dry.

DEAD ON ARRIVAL

Jogging, like cigarettes, is dangerous to your
health. Not everyone who smokes gets cancer, emphy-

sema, or lung disease; however, the percentage is still very high. Likewise, not everyone who jogs will get a coronary or a stroke or any of the other thousands of complications of jogging, but be aware that the percentage is still relatively high. I am not saying that you should give up these crazy strenuous exercises—not unless you want to live a long healthful life. The decision is yours to try. I'd rather walk than die!

Many patients often ask me why we need a cardiologist on hand when we perform a stress electrocardiogram in the hospital. The answer is quite simple. If complications arise from the stress of the exercise electrocardiogram, medical treatment is immediately available. When hospitals first started performing stress EKG's, only a technician was present during the test. After many an unfortunate patient suffered a coronary or died during the procedure, it became mandatory that a cardiologist be present while the test was being performed.

However, no one ever questions the fact that when joggers participate in long distance marathon races, there is no qualified physician or CPR equipment on hand to perform emergency medical treatment if it is needed. One wonders, then, what really is the difference between these two types of activities (the old-time medically unattended stress EKG or a stress marathon race). The end results are often the same: **DEAD ON ARRIVAL!**

ONCE, TWICE, THREE TIMES YOU'RE OUT!

It is now widely known that strenuous exercise can cause sudden death. Cardiac deaths which occur while jogging have been reported with increasing frequency in the past 10 years. Now, if you're lucky enough to survive the hazards of jogging, you may get your chance to die again—*immediately after jogging.*

Post-exercise sudden deaths have now begun to occur frequently, especially after marathon races. Recent studies indicate that during the cool-down phase the joggers' blood pressures dropped dramatically. In order to compensate for this drop in blood pressure, the body pours out large quantities of the hormones norepinephrine and epinephrine. Norepinephrine blood levels can increase to 10 times the normal amount which increases the heart rate and constricts the blood vessels. Epinephrine levels may increase to 3-4 times the normal level, markedly increasing the blood pressure.

This flood of hormones into the bloodstream is actually a reflex effort on the part of the body to restore the blood pressure to normal, following exercise. However, these dangerously high hormone levels may put a fatal strain on the heart, especially in people with underlying coronary artery disease. Researchers suggest that a gradual cool-down phase like **"walking"** following jogging may help to prevent the possibility of post-exercise sudden death.

Did I hear them say walking? Am I nuts? Are they crazy? How many times do you need to be hit on the head to find out that jogging is dangerous? *Once! Twice! Three times, you're out!* Now you not only get the chance to die while you're jogging, but if you manage to survive, you can try again immediately after jogging. And get their nerve! They're trying to salvage their "dead joggers" with my walking program. I won't have it. Either they walk first and finish walking like any intelligent two-legged mammal, or they can finish on all fours—dead or alive!

WALK AWAY AND LIVE ANOTHER DAY

The three basic emotional reactions typical of the so-called **Type A personality** are hostility, impatience and competitiveness. This type of emotional behavior has been shown to be definitely linked to heart disease. The American value system has encouraged people to become achievement-conscious and competitive. This system has led to a stress-oriented society and emotional reactions that contribute to heart disease.

So what do our typical Type A personalities do to combat stress? They run! Now they are competing with other runners, themselves and the clock. They become obsessed with running under the guise of health and try to run faster, further, and better than the time before. Instead of running away from stress, they run smack into it. They literally *run themselves to death.* Instead of decreasing their chance of a heart attack they have actually increased the risk, more than if they had just sat at their desks all day.

Walkers, on the other hand, are non-competitive by nature when exercising. This is not to say that they can't be highly competitive in the workplace; however, they know how to "turn it off." And isn't that the ultimate goal of exercise: to be able to turn off the stress of each day! *Walking is nature's best release valve.* Anxiety, hostility, and anger just float away, and positive, optimistic thoughts replace these stress related feelings. How many times have you been able to solve a difficult problem or deal with a stressful situation after a long refreshing walk. When you feel stress—*walk away, and you will live to face it another day!*

STRESS TESTS MEAN LESS

In a recent study reported in the March 1985 issue of <u>American Health</u> it was found that exercise testing may not be a reliable indicator of coronary artery disease. In one particular study, 43 percent of those patients who had normal stress tests were later found to have coronary artery disease, whereas 22 percent of patients with abnormal stress EKGs were later proved to have no coronary artery disease at all. These false positive and false negative findings have been reported in many similar studies at major medical universities throughout the country over the past 10 years.

What do these results prove? They clearly indicate that a normal stress electrocardiogram is not enough proof that you can start jogging. In fact, many people who have died while jogging had been told that they had no heart disease because of a normal stress EKG. Well then, how can you know for sure if your coronary arteries can take the cruel punishment of jogging? You can't, unless you submit yourself to the potentially dangerous test called "coronary arteriography." This test involves having a plastic catheter inserted into one of your arteries, and then it is pushed through your blood vessels into the coronary arteries surrounding your heart. Then a dye is injected through the catheter and your coronary arteries are outlined on film by the dye. If an obstruction in these arteries is present, it will be revealed on the X-ray pictures. Now you know for sure that you have coronary artery disease and you better not jog.

How many of us would voluntarily submit to such a potentially dangerous test just to find out if we can safely jog? I wouldn't. This test is actually reserved for people who are suspected of having moderate to severe coronary artery disease and may need bypass surgery. Coronary arteriography is essential for these people since it determines which of them can be treated medically and who will need bypass surgery. It certainly is not a test to see who should jog and who shouldn't. However, it is the only test which can tell for certain which of us are at risk from sudden death while jogging or performing strenuous exercises.

What's the answer? It's obvious—**"Walk, Don't Run"** and let your arteries have all the fun. There is enough stress in our lives every day that we have no control over. Why then should we voluntarily try to stress our arteries with such a strenuous, senseless, sadistic pseudo-sport? Remember, sudden death from jogging doesn't happen to all joggers, but the ones it happens to are **100 percent dead**! If you want to avoid coronary bypass surgery, **Walk, Don't Die**, and let the heart surgery *pass you by!*

JOGGING:
THE FINAL NAIL IN ITS COFFIN!

Would you believe that a recent study shows that extreme physical exercise produces bursts of **cancer-causing agents** to be released in the body? Well, it's true, according to a study recently reported at an international meeting sponsored by the University of California and the National Foundation for Cancer Research. These cancer-causing agents are found in small amounts in the body, air, and food; however, they are released in large quantities into the body during vigorous exercise. Experimental animals suffered *tissue and cell damage* when they were exercised vigorously. In addition to the strenuous exercise, other factors which may aid in the release of these harmful agents are a lack of Vitamin E or C.

Now if you're lucky enough to survive all the dangers and hazards of jogging, you may still go down for the final count by developing "jogging cancer." Even though this seems far-fetched and although this study is still in the experimental stage, there's no need to tempt the fates any further. **Walk, Don't Run** and don't let cancer spoil your fun.

"THEY WERE RIGHT WHEN THEY SAID JOGGING WOULD ADD YEARS TO YOUR LIFE. I FEEL TEN YEARS OLDER ALREADY!"

CHAPTER 2

RUNNING ROBOTS & THE LIMPING LAME

RUNNING ROBOTS

Exercise causes the release of a group of chemicals in the brain called **endorphins**, which have a pain-killing effect in addition to their mood-elevating effect. Many runners sustain muscle injuries, ligament tears, and stress fractures while running and never feel them until hours after their exercise. This *analgesic effect* which actually dulls the pain-sense can cause the runner to do irreparable harm to himself because he actually runs through these injuries without actually being aware of them.

Until recently the only way to diagnose stress fractures was by using a *bone scan* because routine x-rays oftentimes would not show these injuries. Most runners after receiving a negative x-ray report would resume running again on the fractured limb until more serious fractures developed. Very few would ever be referred for a bone scan because of the additional expense and the extra radiation entailed. Fortunately for these **running robots**, a new technology has been developed to detect these fractures. The *thermogram* is a device which detects an increased blood supply to the fractured area and appears as a hot spot on the film. The thermogram is considerably lower in cost than a bone scan and has virtually no radiation associated with it.

It somehow seems a shame that we have to resort to x-rays, bone scans, and thermograms, when all we're trying to do is exercise. It might be different if we were professional athletes whose livelihoods depended on strenuous exercise. You don't have to be a running robot with multiple stress fractures to become physically fit. On the contrary, **walking wranglers** are just as fit without the strain, pain or stress fractures. *That's just the breaks!*

THE LIMPING LAME

In a recent study reported in The New England Journal of Medicine, runners who are fanatically committed to exercise may actually be suppressing deep-seated fears of inadequacy. These individuals run despite injuries, personal commitments, or health problems. They will not allow anything whatsoever to interfere with their exercise program and may take a variety of pain and anti-inflammatory drugs with or without prescription to enable them to "limp through life" without stopping. This fact, combined with their obsessive-compulsive personalities, makes these people running time-bombs. According to psychiatrists, joggers' personality traits are similar to anorectics; each hides his fear of inadequacy, and both groups are actually in need of psychotherapy.

JOGGER'S HIGH
CAN MAKE YOU DIE

The brain chemicals (endorphins) which are released during running have an almost morphine-like effect, allowing these runners to tolerate the pain of stress fractures, muscle injuries, torn ligaments and even angina (heart pain). Heart attacks and sudden deaths in runners may be related to the runner's inability to feel pain while running because of the analgesic effect of these endorphins. Ordinarily a heart attack victim has the warning signs of chest pain or shortness of breath and will usually seek medical treatment promptly. The jogger who has reached the so-called "jogger's high" or "jogger's euphoria" may not be able to feel this pain until it is too late. *Walk, Don't Die* and you'll avoid this high.

OH MY ACHING BACK!

At one time or another most of us will have a painful backache. There are several common causes of backaches: poor posture, bending or lifting incorrectly, inactivity, stress and tension, or just being overweight. Other more serious causes of low back pain include arthritis, disc disease, osteoporosis, back injuries and congenital abnormalities.

No matter what the cause, except for the more serious disorders, *walking* is universally accepted as the one exercise which helps heal and strengthen a back problem. Once the initial treatment is completed to relieve the painful muscle spasm that accompanies most back disorders, walking is the safest exercise to strengthen weak back muscles.

Studies show that regular walkers have less backaches and back problems in general than non-walkers. And once having had a back problem, walkers by and large have fewer recurrences of back pain. Jogging, on the other hand, is probably the worst form of exercise for a bad back, since it produces undue stress and strain on the back's ligaments, discs, and vertebrae. *"Back-off from that run or you'll be back on your back."*

THE LEGS ARE THE FIRST TO GO

Osteoarthritis is a condition which eventually affects the majority of people over 60. The knees are often the first joints to be affected. Several recent studies show that people who walk regularly have less pain, greater flexibility and less joint inflammation than sedentary people. **Walking** and the **stationary bike** are the most suitable exercises for this condition since they put less pressure on the knees and ankles than strenuous exercises or calisthenics.

Jogging and deep knee bends are by far the worst forms of exercise for this condition. This type of exercise puts undue pressure on the ligaments and cartilages of the ankle, knee and hip joints. This continued trauma results in chronic inflammation of the joints, leading eventually to osteoarthritis. The joints become inflamed, swollen, painful, and lose their mobility. Strenuous exercises only tend to aggravate the arthritis.

The incidence of **osteoarthritis** in runners is approximately 15.5 percent as compared to 0.1 percent for the general population. Although osteoarthritis is one of the conditions that affects many people over the age of 60, its incidence is relatively low in younger population groups. The mean age of runners affected with osteoarthritis is 47.8 years—approximately 13 years earlier than the general population. The incidence is related directly to the total number of years and the distance these runners ran each week. More miles and more years combined to produce more arthritis as a result of the continued trauma to the legs, hips and back.

Walking, on the other hand, does not cause arthritis and it can actually benefit people who have already developed certain forms of arthritis. Recent studies indicate that the moderate stimulation of arthritic joints by walking induced cartilage cells in the joints to grow, which helped to heal the damaged joint. In a study of 280 people over the age of 65 with moderate arthritis, a walking program helped these patients regain mobility in the ankle, knee, and hip joints.

Walking with properly fitted shoes with a thick crepe sole absorbs the shock of the surface walked on before it gets to the ankles, knees and hips. Stationary cycling takes the weight of the body off the ankles and knees and lessens the strain on these joints and ligaments. A walking program will keep your legs limber for a lifetime. Remember, the more that strenuous exercise is done, the worse the legs become. You don't want your legs to go before you do. *Walk, Don't Run* and let your legs have some fun!

STICKS AND STONES WILL BREAK YOUR BONES AND SO WILL JOGGING

In a recent study presented at an American College of Sports Medicine meeting, orthopedic injuries in the lower extremities were found to have occurred at a significantly higher percentage in runners as compared to non-runners. Medical histories on over 2,500 middle-aged healthy males (1,837 runners and 693 non-runners) were followed over a 6 year period. The following percentage of comparison injuries were reported as follows:

	RUNNERS	NON-RUNNERS
HIP INJURIES	1.44%	0.44%
FOOT INJURIES	5.94%	2.49%
KNEE INJURIES	5.60%	1.22%

JOGGER'S JEOPARDY

Recent research has confirmed what most wives of joggers already knew—joggers are lousy lovers. This survey showed that the typical couple cut lovemaking in half once the husband started jogging while others decreased the frequency by three-quarters.

The reason is easy to figure out. These joggers were literally too pooped to pop. They were so fatigued that they were devoid of any emotion. A recent Canadian study revealed that strenuous exercise, especially jogging, caused a 30-40% drop in the male sex hormone, *testosterone*. This hormone is necessary for normal male sexual function.

Similar studies on women long-distance runners have also found a similar reduction of the female sex hormones. In many cases these women not only experienced a reduction in sex drive but also a complete cessation of menstruation.

DIRTY DOZEN DANGERS DOUBLED

There have been over 1,500 different types of injuries and disabilities reported as a result of jogging. Listed below are just two dozen of the thousands of reported dangers and hazards directly related to jogging.

1. *Pregnant joggers* should be cautious about strenuous exercise due to the shunting of oxygenated blood (blood with a full load of oxygen) to the periphery (the muscles used in exercise). This may result in some poorly oxygenated blood circulating to the developing embryo, which could result in birth defects.

2. Many women who take up jogging note that after a short period of time due to the rapid weight loss, they *stop menstruating* temporarily. This occurs because of the production of a substance called beta-endorphin which suppresses the female hormones regulating the menstrual cycle and subsequently stops ovulation. These women actually exhibit symptoms of early menopause. They become

anemic and they also lose calcium from their bones, which may lead to osteoporosis. These conditions are usually reversible once the women stop jogging. Recent studies, however, have linked permanent infertility with ovarian damage, which was caused by a lack of blood supply to the ovaries during strenuous exercise.

3. *Traffic injuries and accidents* are becoming an ever increasing hazard to the roadside jogger. These accidents occur more frequently at dusk, in the evening, or when the weather is bad because of poor visibility. Joggers who wear dark clothing are at even greater risk.

4. *Morton's Metatàrsalgia,* which is defined as a persistent pain in the nerve between the toes, can occur in individuals who have a second toe longer than the big toe. During running, by constantly jamming this toe against the front of the shoe or sneaker, the injury results in nerve damage. Many such cases require surgical treatment.

5 During running *small hemorrhages* and swelling may develop underneath the toe nails, which results from trauma and a lack of blood supply. These hemorrhages may cause the loss of the toenails. In most cases these toenails regenerate once the individual has stopped running.

6. *Runner's nipple* is a common phenomenon noted in both male and female runners. The condition is a result of abrading the nipples against the shirt which eventually causes bleeding and inflammation or infection.

7. Many physicians have been noting increased cases of a type of arthritis known as *osteoarthritis,* in the ankles, knees and hips of runners. This type of arthritis is caused by an inflammation and thickening of the bone and cartilage of the joints. It is thought that the stress from running imposed on these body-supporting joints leads to this form of arthritis, which in many cases can be permanent.

8. *Tendonitis* is one of the most common injuries sustained by runners, especially in the tendons of the feet and ankles. During running, severe stress produces tiny tears, sprains and strains in these small tendons, which become inflamed and result in pain. One of the most common types of tendon injuries are "shin splints," which result from tiny tears or pulls of the tendons attaching the shin muscles to the bone. Tendonitis of the long bones of the feet produces painful swelling on the top of the foot. Heel-bone tendonitis and bone spurs can also result from jogging. Ankle tendonitis (Achilles tendonitis) may require surgery if this tendon ruptures.

9. *Hairline fractures* of the small bones of the feet and on occasion the small bone of the lower leg (fibula) are becoming more apparent. These fractures are caused by stress, over-abuse and over-. use of the legs. These tiny stress fractures will heal once the runner stops running; however, since many runners run with pain in their legs or feet, these tiny stress fractures can become full blown fractures requiring plaster casts.

10. Many people are born with *congenital malalignments* of the ankles, knees, or hips. These minor malalignments will not interfere with normal activities such as walking. However, they do become more apparent during running and tend to produce more running-type injuries. One of the more common malalignment types of injury results in a *painful wobbly kneecap* (chondromalacia patella) which becomes worse with running.

11. *Anterior Tibial Compartment Syndrome*—This condition results from muscle swelling which occurs in a group of muscles encased in a compartment or sheath (fascia) near the shin bone. When the muscles swell and the sheath does not yield, there is pain caused by the pressure of the muscles against the fascia. If this pain is ignored, the mus-

cles could permanently lose their blood supply, leading to muscle damage and paralysis. This condition often requires surgery to open or remove the fascia and allow the muscles to expand.

12. *Groin injuries* are rather common and are caused by striding longer with one leg than the other, with subsequent pulls on the groin muscle. If you are right-handed then you are probably also right legged and you will stride out longer with the right leg, and subsequently pull the groin muscle in the opposite leg.

13. Runners have earned themselves a special term for their pains—*runner's knee.* Since the knee takes more stress than other joints in running, it is particularly prone to injury. The cartilage under the kneecap first becomes bruised when running. Then the cartilage begins to soften and get mushy causing chronic pain in the knee even with walking. This condition can progress to a chronic inflammation of the knee joint leading to arthritis and an instability of the kneecap often requiring surgery.

14. *Retinal and vitreous detachments* secondary to jogging have been reported to occur in susceptible individuals. The pounding effect of jogging may contribute to detaching the retina in the eye, leading to blindness, if not corrected promptly by surgery or laser treatments.

15. Several cases of potentially fatal *allergic reactions* known as anaphylactic shock have occurred in well conditioned runners during exercise. These attacks begin with itching and redness of the skin, followed by hives and swelling and later followed by nausea, chest tightness, irregular heartbeat, difficult breathing and low blood pressure. The cause of this allergic type of *exercise-induced asthma* is not known; however, it is suggested that these individuals suffer from other allergies and the exercise-type reaction is triggered by inhaling

or eating certain allergic substances prior to running.

16. Joggers who exercise repeatedly on heavily trafficked roads or city streets have an increased level of *carbon monoxide* in the blood from the exhaust fumes from these automobiles and trucks. Carbon monoxide is very dangerous to the heart and nervous tissues since it attaches itself to the hemoglobin portion of the blood and removes the oxygen from those blood cells. Joggers who have minor respiratory ailments suffer the most when running in bad air.

17. *Heat exhaustion* occurs frequently in runners because of the double heat load in summer created by raising the body temperature from high humidity and radiant heat from sunlight. Heat exhaustion can result in muscle cramps and twitches, blurred vision, excessive thirst, fatigue, loss of coordination and a sudden drop in blood pressure. *Heatstroke* is a life-threatening complication resulting from exercising in hot humid weather. Joggers because of their high levels of endorphins, do not feel the dangerous effects of heat until it is often too late. These runners then may suffer heatstroke resulting in a sudden drop in blood pressure, circulatory collapse, coma and death if it is not treated promptly. The incidence of deaths from heatstroke in young adults is second only to deaths from head and spine auto injuries.

18. In a recent study, scientists have discovered an increased level of a group of chemicals called *prostaglandins* in the blood of joggers. These chemicals can produce symptoms of nausea, vomiting, lightheadedness, diarrhea, cramps, fatigue and even elevated blood pressure.

19. In another study on hormone levels in runners, it was recently discovered that increased levels of a chemical agent called *dopamine*, which is related to the chemical group endorphins, also has a natu-

ral sedative and analgesic effect on the brain. This would account for the euphoria that many runners experience and contributes to runners being unaware of injuries that they have sustained while running, such as stress fractures of the small bones of the feet and painless heart attacks resulting in sudden death.

20. *Hypoglycemia* (a sudden drop in blood sugar) may result from running long distances without adequate fluid intake. This can result in sweating, tremors, nausea, mental confusion and marked weakness. *Hypovolemic collapse* is a more severe type of reaction seen in runners who have not taken in enough fluids before and during their races. These runners develop nausea, vomiting, diarrhea, a weak pulse and drop in blood pressure, a bluish discoloration of the face and neck (cyanosis) and finally shock and fainting. The condition is usually self-limiting once the individual has been treated with intravenous fluids.

21. *Potassium depletion* occurs frequently in runners especially in warm weather. Potassium is lost both through the sweat and the urine. This loss of potassium can result in muscle cramps, dizziness, palpitations and heart rhythm irregularities.

22. *Sports anemia* is a condition which occurs from the pounding of the feet on hard surfaces. This impact causes the red blood cells to break down and be excreted in the urine. If enough blood cells are broken down the urine turns red. The blood count in this condition actually shows that the runner is anemic (low in total red blood cells and iron content).

23. Another cause of *blood in the urine* is the jarring of the bladder against the pelvic bones when jogging. The bladder wall actually gets bruised and bleeds into the urine. A more severe cause of blood in the urine may result when the kidneys don't get enough blood supply during running. When com-

bined with dehydration this may result in permanent kidney damage.

24. *Penile frostbite* and *jogger's genitals* have also been reported. Frostbite is a result of running without adequate clothing in cold weather. Jogger's genitals is an inflammation of the prostate gland caused by the extreme gravitation pull on the prostate gland by the force of jogging. *Hypothermia* (the body's inner temperature drops below normal) is a rare, often fatal complication, which may result from running in extremely cold weather without adequate clothing. The body is unable to generate adequate heat and the runner collapses from exhaustion and low body temperature.

*   *   *   *   *   *   *   *

Of the 16,000 runners participating in the 1985 New York City Marathon more than 1,200 sought medical care at or near the finish line. One runner every 4 minutes was admitted to an on-site acute treatment area and 209 runners actually required treatment at New York City area hospitals. And listed among these statistics was a small note indicating that "there was only one death in this year's marathon— Jacques Bussereau, 48, of France, of heart attack." I had to read the report twice to see if anyone could actually be that casual about reporting the death of an apparently healthy man. Does this sound like an exercise for health and fitness? It seems to me that this is a crash-course in self-destruction. I guess it's nature's way of dealing with the over-population crisis.

Casualties were reported as "light" in this year's Boston Marathon (4-21-86). There were "only" 700 to 800 injuries sustained compared to 1500 casualties in 1985. And get this—only 18 people required hospitalization and no deaths were reported in this year's marathon. If that's what they call "light casualties", I'd hate to be there on a bad day!

OTHER JOGGING JEOPARDIES

Musculo-Skeletal System: Muscle cramps and sprains, ligament and tendon injuries, cartilage tears and bone dislocations. Stress fractures (bones of feet, long bones of leg, pelvis, hip, and spinal vertebrae). Also arthritis flare-ups and back injuries.

Nervous System: Compressed nerves in the neck, arms, legs and low back resulting in pain, numbness and weakness. Slipped discs resulting in nerve damage.

Metabolic System: Chemical imbalances in the blood (ex. calcium and potassium loss), and blood sugar abnormalities.

Immune System: Itching and redness of skin, hives and swelling, and anaphylaxis (shock, swelling, irregular heartbeat—sometimes leading to death).

Obstetrics and Gynecology: Menstrual irregularities, miscarriages, birth defects, prolapse (dropping) of the uterus and ovarian damage.

Renal System: Blood and protein in the urine, bladder bruises, kidney damage and prolapse of bladder.

Cardiovascular System: Palpitations, chest pain, heartbeat abnormalities, heart attacks and sudden death. Hypertension and strokes from ruptured arteries in the brain (aneurysms).

Respiratory System: Shortness of breath, fatigue, wheezing, exercise-induced asthma, partial lung collapse (pneumothorax) and respiratory failure.

Gastrointestinal System: Abdominal cramps, nausea, vomiting, stress ulcers of stomach and bloody diarrhea (caused by decreased blood supply to the colon).

The Eye: Inflammation, irritation, conjunctivitis, vitreous hemorrhages and retinal detachments.

Environmental: Frostbite, heat exhaustion, heatstroke, hypothermia, dogbites, auto accidents and lung damage from polluted air.

Psychiatric: Anxiety, depression and obsessive-compulsive behavior (running mania).

Endocrine (Hormone) System: Decreased sex drive, impotence, infertility, menstrual abnormalities, adrenal and thyroid gland disorders. Also ovarian and testicular damage from poor blood supply.

CHAPTER 3

THE CASE OF THE JANGLED JOGGER

ALL I WANT
ARE THE FACTS, MA'AM

There are three major effects that exercise has on the circulatory system, so that it can supply the tremendous amount of blood required by the muscles during exercise. These are the facts:

1. SYMPATHETIC NERVOUS SYSTEM STIMULATES CIRCULATION

At the onset of exercise, signals from the brain and the sympathetic nervous system stimulate the heart to greatly increase its activity.

Next, all the blood vessels of the peripheral circulation (the non-exercising parts of the body) are strongly constricted—in other words, their small arteries narrow down and the blood flow is reduced to these non-muscular areas.

Then the blood vessels of the active exercising

muscles widen (dilate). This provides an increased flow of blood in order to supply more oxygen to these exercising muscles.

The heart is stimulated to beat faster, to supply this increased flow of blood required by the exercising muscles. The blood supply through most of the non-muscular areas of the body is temporarily reduced (shut-off)—in effect, they are lending their blood supply to the active muscles.

Fortunately for us, our hearts and brains have better workmanship than the rest of our organs. Neither one will just stand around in line like the rest of the peasants (liver, kidneys, stomach, etc.) patiently waiting for their allotment of oxygen. The rest of the non-exercising parts of the body constrict (narrow) their arteries during exercise, so that the exercising muscles which dilate (open) their blood vessels can get more blood and oxygen. However, the arteries of the heart and brain do not narrow or constrict during exercise since these arteries are not under the control of the sympathetic nervous system. Whoever designed the human body was smart enough to realize that if these arteries narrowed down every time you got up from your chair, you wouldn't live long enough to walk across the room.

Does this mean that the heart and brain don't suffer any ill effects from strenuous exercise? **Definitely not!** All it means is that the heart and brain are too smart to allow themselves to be deprived of their fair share of oxygen before, during and after exercise. But unfortunately, they can suffer other ill effects from strenuous exercise which are unrelated to their ability to extract oxygen. These ill effects can be seen when we discuss the next two major effects that exercise has on the circulatory system.

2. INCREASED CARDIAC OUTPUT

The cardiac output is defined as the quantity of blood pumped out by the left ventricle (chamber) of the heart into the aorta (main artery leaving the heart) each minute. The tremendous increase in the cardiac output that occurs during exercise results from the increased quantity of blood which was sent to the exercising muscles and which is promptly returned to the heart by way of the veins. The heart, in turn, rapidly pumps out this blood after re-oxygenation in the lungs, and sends it back immediately to the muscles by way of the arteries. The heart rate begins to increase and the heart muscle contracts more vigorously with each beat.

The ability of the trained athlete to increase his cardiac output, in order to deliver oxygen and nutrients to the cells of his body, is actually what determines the amount of prolonged heavy exercise that he can sustain. This is what is commonly called *physical fitness—not good health!* They are two entirely different things.

If the person who is training for physical fitness has any underlying, undiagnosed heart disease, then his heart will not perform like a trained seal. In fact, by increasing the cardiac output in an unhealthy heart you are playing with a loaded gun. The unhealthy heart can do one of three things if it is stressed beyond its limit:

1. It can beat irregularly causing **heart failure!**
2. Its blood supply can be shut off because of narrowed coronary arteries causing a **heart attack!**
3. Or it can just stop—**cardiac arrest!**

There is only one thing that the unhealthy heart *can't* do with strenuous exercise and that's—*get better!* Damaged or unhealthy hearts need supervised medical attention either in the form of diet, medication, mild-moderate exercise, and in some cases, surgery. In my 25 years as a practicing physician I have never seen or heard any qualified physician recommend masochistic, barbaric, back-breaking, heart-pounding strenuous exercises to heal a sick heart.

3. INCREASED BLOOD PRESSURE

The blood vessels of the rest of the non-exercising part of the body (liver, spleen, kidneys, intestinal tract, etc.) constrict or narrow down during exercise. This offers a certain amount of resistance to the heart pumping out blood, and is known as the *peripheral resistance*. This resistance to the flow of blood through the tissues where the arteries are constricted causes the blood pressure to rise. The arteries, however, that supply the exercising muscles dilate, and this helps to lower the peripheral resistance and prevents the blood pressure from going up too high.

The only problem that can arise is when a person pushes himself too fast and too far as in heavy strenuous exercise. The rapid increase in the *cardiac output* and the rapid increase in the *peripheral resistance* can cause the blood pressure to soar to dangerous levels. The heart can enlarge over a period of time from such strain, just like it does in untreated cases of hypertension, leading in some cases to heart failure. No one has ever convinced me that an enlarged heart in an athlete is a normal condition. An enlarged heart acts the same no matter whose body you put it into—it has to work harder than a normal sized heart and it will give out faster over the long run, possibly leading to heart failure.

The blood pressure during strenuous exercise can rise to such high levels as to precipitate heart attacks and strokes in patients with underlying heart and artery disease. There are some people who have a congenital weakness in an artery (aneurysm) in their brain. With strenuous exercise this artery may rupture, similar to a blowout on a tire, causing a brain hemorrhage. Does any of this sound like the road to good health? Not to me. The only safe, effective, sure way to good health and fitness is to see your doctor for regular checkups. Let him examine you thoroughly with his trained eye and **Walk Don't Die!**

A MURDER MYSTERY: AND THEN THERE WERE NONE

BODY MANSION

Walking is an **aerobic exercise** second to none. It produces exactly the same health, fitness and weight control benefits as other strenuous activities at 1/1000 the risk. The cardiovascular benefits are exactly the same without the strain or pain. Aerobic exercise is defined as the type of exercise in which the oxygen demand of the large muscles of the body does not exceed the oxygen supply. Walking, which is the ultimate aerobic exercise, is designed to increase endurance and produces what is called the *training effect* which improves cardiovascular fitness.

The main function of aerobic exercise then is to supply **oxygen** to all the **cells in your body's mansion**. This oxygen then reacts with glucose (blood sugar) in order to produce **energy**. Some of the energy thus produced is used immediately by the body to form heat and to be used in essential chemical reactions. The rest of the energy so produced is stored in tiny packets of energy (ATP) to be used later when needed.

This chemical reaction in which oxygen combines with blood sugar to produce energy is a relatively slow reaction; therefore, each individual body cell (liver, kidney, intestinal tract, and other organs) can extract only so much oxygen at a time from the bloodstream to carry on what is called *cellular metabolism*. During aerobic exercise a good bit of the oxygen is picked up by the exercising muscles (legs, arms, chest wall and respiratory muscles); however, plenty of oxygen is still left over for use by the rest of the cells living in your body's mansion.

BLACKMAIL: OXYGEN DEBT

When the exercise gets too strenuous (ex: jogging), the exercising muscles begin to use up and require more and more oxygen. There eventually comes a point when these exercising muscles cannot actually get enough oxygen. This point at which the oxygen demand exceeds the oxygen supply produces a condition known as **oxygen debt**. At this stage aerobic exercise becomes **anaerobic exercise** (without oxygen).

Now what does all this mean? In strenuous muscular exercise (jogging) where you can't breathe in enough oxygen to satisfy the requirements of your muscles, a chemical reaction occurs in which the muscles try to squeeze out some more energy without using oxygen. This is known as **anaerobic metabolism** (without oxygen) and it is actually a trick that the body uses to get a little extra energy without oxygen being available.

VILLAINS DEMAND PAYOFF!

There are two catches, however, to this slight-of-hand trick (anaerobic metabolism) that our body uses to produce energy without using oxygen. The first is that your body must break down small particles of *muscle starch* (glycogen) to squeeze out their extra energy. The price it pays to do this is that when you break down muscle starch you produce a rather nasty chemical villain called **lactic acid**. This lactic acid builds up in your muscles causing muscle cramps at first and then profound muscle weakness. Then severe muscle fatigue forces you to stop exercising.

We now come to the second catch of anaerobic metabolism. You still owe oxygen (oxygen debt) to these **villainous exercising muscles** that have been running without gas (oxygen) on fumes alone. And you must get rid of the **other villain—lactic acid** that has built up in your muscles.

This oxygen debt is paid back during the *immediate recovery period* following exercise. As soon as you stop exercising, you automatically begin to **pant** (breathe rapidly and deeply). The excess oxygen that you now take in supplies the muscles with the oxygen that they couldn't previously get during the strenuous exercise. You are in a sense *paying-off the oxygen debt* now. And the additional oxygen taken in is also used to *remove the lactic acid* from the muscles and to replenish the stored little packets of energy (ATP) which were depleted during the period of oxygen debt.

THE MURDER PLOT

Now you're saying, that's nice but what does all this have to do with a murder. Well, I had to introduce the cast of characters with a little basic physiology first, so that you won't come in at the end of the movie and not know who the suspects are in the murder mystery.

Remember way back in the mystery plot when we talked about the **little body cells** (liver, kidney, intestinal tract and other organs) patiently taking their little share of oxygen from the bloodstream to carry on their household duties (metabolism). And remember that I said that when we walk (aerobic exercise) the muscles use more oxygen than they normally use, but there is still plenty of oxygen left over for our little friends (the body cells).

What we didn't know at the time was that during strenuous anaerobic exercise (jogging, etc.) these little friendly body cells from our organs started to choke a little because the jogger's muscles began to demand more and more oxygen. And the more they got, the more they needed until a point was reached when the cells of the body that were not engaged in the actual exercise (ex: liver, spleen, kidneys, intestinal tract and so on) began to be unable to get enough oxygen from the blood because of the big exercising muscle hogs who wanted it all. The supply of oxygen was actually shunted away from these non-exercising organs in order to supply the exercising muscles' insatiable appetite for oxygen.

And to make matters even worse, when the jogger stops jogging, he rapidly breathes (pants) to get in enough oxygen to pay off his oxygen debt. Guess who gets first crack at the new supply of oxygen? The starved little friendly liver, kidney, spleen and intestinal cells—not a chance! The big exercising muscle gluttons again hog all the new-found oxygen pouring through the bloodstream, so that they can rapidly pay off their oxygen debt.

Now you see that the plot thickens. These little body cells get stood up twice. First, when the strenuous exercise reaches the anaerobic stage they get short-changed on their supply of oxygen. Secondly, after the exercise is stopped and the jogger breathes in more oxygen to pay off the oxygen debt, our trusting little starved body cells wait patiently with their mouths open to receive their supply of oxygen. So what happens, the exercising muscle pigs gobble it all up to pay off their oxygen debt. *Who ever said that life was fair!*

THE MURDER VICTIMS

Let's take the first victim—**your kidneys**! Have you heard about joggers who get blood in their urine—

well this can occur when the kidneys do not get enough oxygen during jogging and this may result in a condition known as *ischemia* (lack of blood supply). Marathon runners who get severely dehydrated and suffer a lack of oxygen to their kidneys, have been known to develop a severe kidney disorder called *tubular necrosis* (death of kidney tissue). A more common cause of blood in the urine occurs when joggers' bladders get bumped around in their pelvises. This cause of blood in the urine, however, is a relatively common benign self-limiting condition—no murder actually occurs here.

Victim number two is your **intestinal tract**! Ever hear about runners getting severe abdominal cramps or bloody diarrhea? This is again caused by a lack of oxygen and blood supply to the intestines. There have been actual cases where sections of the intestinal tract have actually died from a lack of blood supply, a condition known as *ischemic necrosis*. Surgery was necessary in these cases to remove the dead portion of intestine.

Victims number three, four, five, and six are your **liver**, **spleen**, **pancreas**, and **adrenal glands**. Lack of proper blood supply and oxygen to these vital organs has been reported on rare occasions to cause small hemorrhages (infarcts) in the organs themselves causing actual tissue death. Usually no permanent damage to these vital organs occurs; however, if enough of the organ is damaged by a lack of blood supply, then the function of that particular organ may be seriously impaired.

What about our two smart organs—the **heart** and **brain**? They were too clever to fall for this decreased oxygen game. They made sure they got their oxygen allotments no matter how fast the muscle gluttons gobbled up the extra oxygen. They weren't going to be murder victims numbers seven and eight. Or were they?

These two smart cookies (heart and brain) certainly weren't going to fall victim to the deadly exercising muscles' plot, as did the poor kidneys, liver, stomach and other body cells. But guess what? When the two of them weren't looking, another murderer was lurking in Body Mansion. This silent killer lurked stealthily in the shadows. And at the right moment when the jogger was going full steam—bang! He blew them both away.

Who was this silent murderer? How did he do it? Where did he come from? Who in the world would have ever thought that all these unlikely inhabitants of Body Mansion, were to become murder victims in a diabolical plot by a master criminal? Only one man would be able to solve this murder mystery, none other than the world's greatest detective, Sherlock Holmes. Let's peek into his drawing room and listen as he solves *"The Case of the Jangled Jogger."*

SHERLOCK HOLMES AND THE CASE OF THE JANGLED JOGGER

As Sherlock Holmes sat peacefully smoking his old brier-root pipe, Dr. Watson broke into his thoughts by saying, "Surely, Holmes, this medical report has nothing whatsoever to do with the case."

"What case my dear fellow?" said Holmes.

"Why the case of the multiple jogger murders," responded Watson angrily.

"Oh, that case," said Holmes humorously, "I was just pulling your leg, Watson. Actually, I was deep in thought when you so rudely interrupted me. The fact of the matter is, Watson, that the inhabitants of Body Mansion must all be viewed with a jaundiced eye. A little background information into their personal lives is essential to the successful conclusion of a most singular case such as this my dear fellow."

"Take for instance the two most likely suspects: the villainous lactic acid or the suave well-built exercising muscles. One would leap at the obvious guilt of both these treacherous criminals. And yet, Watson, I feel that the case is not quite so simple as that. In fact, my dear fellow, I think these two likely suspects have been planted as red herrings in an attempt to throw me off the track. I'll not have it Watson. This murderous fiend must be apprehended and I can feel his hot breath close at hand."

"*Come, Watson, come!*" he cried. "*The game is afoot.*"[1]

"We must make haste before he takes yet another life. We'll do well to keep a wide berth, my good man, for I feel we are close at hand and may surprise him in his lair."

"But Holmes," cried Watson, "is it wise to try and trap a dangerous criminal without proper precautions? Shouldn't we call chief-inspector Lestrade?"

"*My dear fellow, you know my methods.*"[2]

"There's no time, Watson, if we let on that we suspect him, he may again slip through our net, and I fear we may never have another chance such as this."

"But who is the murderer, Holmes?" Watson persisted.

"You must apply my precepts Watson," he said, shaking his head. "*How often have I said to you that when you have eliminated the impossible, whatever remains, however improbable, must be the truth?*"[3]

"But Holmes, even the police with all of their resources haven't a clue to the murderer's identity," insisted Watson.

"*It is a capital mistake to theorize before one has*

---

[1] Sir Arthur Conan Doyle, "The Abbey Grange," in *The Return of Sherlock Holmes* (London: George Newnes, 1905).

---

[2] Sir Arthur Conan Doyle, "The Stockbroker's Clerk," in *The Memoirs of Sherlock Holmes* (London: George Newnes, 1894).

---

[3] Sir Arthur Conan Doyle, *The Sign of Four* (Philadelphia: J. B. Lippincott, 1890).

data. Insensibly one begins to twist facts to suit theories, instead of theories to suit facts."[4]

"Lactic acid and the exercising muscles were mere tools, henchmen in fact, for this master criminal. He used both of them for his own means as a painter would use a brush and his canvas." *"You can tell an old master by the sweep of his brush, Watson."*[5]

"Well, this mass murderer cleverly killed these joggers, Watson, by actually bursting their hearts or by exploding their brains. It was as if, Watson, he pulled the trigger of the exercising muscles' gun and blamed the muscles for the actual murder. Remember it was this silent killer who induced the joggers to run, Watson, and it is he who must pay for this dastardly deed."

"The exercising muscles and lactic acid were but mere pawns in his overall deadly game. They were left at the scene of the murder to pay for his crimes. And caught red-handed, they were helpless to defend themselves, for remember, Watson, they both were mute and could produce no witnesses who would vouch for them. A decidedly clever crime, Watson, for this fiend is a master criminal second to none."

"He is the Napoleon of crime, Watson."[6]

"He spins his spider's web in a thousand places and not one crime has been brought to bear against him, save this one. We have won, Watson, and good riddance to the fellow—he is a decidedly bad lot, although a more brilliant criminal genius has yet to be born that can compare to this Machiavellian murderer."

---

[4] Sir Arthur Conan Doyle, "A Scandel in Bohemia," *The Adventures of Sherlock Holmes* (New York: Harper and Brothers, 1892).

---

[5] Sir Arthur Conan Doyle, *The Valley of Fear* (London: Smith, Elder, 1915).

---

[6] Sir Arthur Conan Doyle, "The Final Problem," in *The Memoirs of Sherlock Holmes* (London: George Newnes, 1894).

"But Holmes, who is the murderer and how on earth did you get on to him with so few clues?"

"You know my method. It is founded upon the observation of trifles."[7]

"The most singular clue in this case, Watson, was the fact that each and every dead jogger was found wearing a particularly uncommon brand of jogging shoe and a rather expensive designer sweat-suit, neither of which are to be found in this part of London. And what say you Watson, to the fact that both the shoes and the sweat-suits were one and all monogrammed with a most singular emblem, consisting of the capital letter "M" surrounded by a most peculiar complex mathematical equation. And who, pray tell, runs the most expensive and elaborate fitness centers on the outskirts of London, my dear Watson? Think carefully, my good fellow, whose name begins with an "M" and has written a mathematical treatise on the Binomial Theorem? Why of course, Watson, our monogram murderer is none other than Professor James Moriarty!"

"Our old arch enemy, Professor Moriarty, the sadistic fitness fiend, is in reality the actual murderer, Watson. He sent his legion of jangled joggers to and fro to do his bidding. These mindless beggars were merely running robots used deviously to perform his many crimes. And what save, Watson, but a few thousand deaths among this army of jangled joggers. He had thousands more, waiting in the wings to take their place, for he dangled false treasures in their eyes."

"What do you mean, Holmes, by saying he had so many others to take the place of the dead joggers? And what treasures did he promise them?"

"It's obvious, Watson, to anyone but a fool that these jangled joggers were in jeopardy. Think careful-

---

[7] Sir Arthur Conan Doyle, "The Bascombe Valley Mystery," in *The Adventures of Sherlock Holmes* (New York: Harper and Brothers, 1892).

ly, my good fellow, and use your wits to reason the problem carefully. Remember what I've taught you, Watson, about careful observation and deduction leading to the correct solution."

"What possible inducements do you think Moriarty made to these jangled joggers, Watson?"

"I have no idea," admitted Watson.

"Why he promised them the four things that everyone wants—weight-loss, fitness, good health and long life," said Holmes sarcastically. "And what did he do Watson? He sent them to their deaths—one by one they dropped over. They one and all thought they were helping themselves to obtain fitness and good health. And in reality they were literally jumping to their own deaths."

" 'Run here, run there,' he would tell them, and these poor souls would do his bidding without question. 'You'll be as fit as a fiddle,' he told them. 'Lose weight, keep fit, stay healthy, live longer,' he would tell them. And not a word of truth in it Watson. These jangled joggers believed everything he told them because he was the so-called foremost authority on fitness and weight-loss in England. Never did they stop and reason what they were doing. If Moriarty said running was good for them, they ran. And in the end, Watson, they literally ran their hearts out for him. Their poor hearts couldn't take the strain, Watson, and they died one by one."

"When these exhausted souls would ask about their friends who had dropped dead, Moriarty would say—'an isolated case my friend, don't worry, it can't happen to you.' And when the league of jangled joggers broke bone after bone, tore ligament after ligament and suffered a thousand injuries, he would say 'It's the price we must pay for fitness, my good men.' He cared not one farthing for their well-being, Watson. His only concern was that they do his bidding without question while he sat quietly in his spider's web and manipulated their lives."

"But Holmes," cried Watson, "what was his reason, what was his purpose in all this?"

"Crime is common. Logic is rare. Therefore, it is upon the logic rather than upon the crime that you should dwell,[8] my dear Watson."

"Think, man, think!" exclaimed Holmes. "Why what else but power and money. He became rich and famous from this league of jangled joggers. They would beg, borrow and steal so that they could pay their monthly health club dues in order to be a member of his famous band of joggers. He supplied them with designer sweatsuits and monogrammed shoes and operated slick fitness centers for which they paid dearly. But in the end Watson these poor souls paid more than money, they paid with their lives."

"There's only one thing I don't understand Holmes."

"Only one thing my good man, I find that hard to believe."

"Now, Holmes don't be sarcastic."

"There is a delightful freshness about you, Watson, which makes it a pleasure to exercise any small powers which I may possess at your expense.[9] You must forgive me my dear fellow, proceed and ask your little question."

"Well Holmes, why on earth were most of these jangled joggers Americans?"

"Good show, Watson, I thought you'd never catch on. The reason, my fine friend, is that Americans by and large are basically a rather insecure, masochistic lot. They think that if a thing is difficult to do and if it is painful, then it must necessarily be a good thing.

---

[8] Sir Arthur Conan Doyle, "The Copper Beeches," in *The Adventures of Sherlock Holmes* (New York: Harper and Brothers, 1892).

---

[9] Sir Arthur Conan Doyle, *The Hound of the Baskervilles* (London: George Newnes, 1902).

The bloody beggars are built that way Watson, and you can't even breed it out of them. Moriarty played on this defect, Watson, by giving them what they wanted—a set of crippling calisthenics and a strenuous running program which set these jangled joggers on their heels. The poor devils never knew what hit them, Watson, for they dropped like flies, one by one."

"But Holmes, why did so many of the joggers die in the first place?"

Why that should be obvious to you, being a medical man, my dear fellow. These poor wretches hadn't done a stitch of exercise in 20 years, and besides, many of them had underlying hypertension and heart disease."

"The solution seems so simple when you explain it Holmes."

"*Every problem becomes very childish when once it is explained to you,*[10] my dear fellow."

"If these poor souls had followed your precepts, Watson, and walked rather than jogged, they would still be alive today." "And speaking of walking Watson, you know that, *'I get so little active exercise that it is always a treat,'*[11] to take a brisk walk with you."

"The mystery of the Jangled Jogger was certainly one of your most difficult and yet most memorable cases, Holmes."

"*There is no branch of detective science which is so important and so much neglected as the art of tracing footsteps.*[12] In this particular case Watson, there was the singular clue of the monogrammed footprint. What could be easier, my dear fellow?"

"Amazing, Holmes!"

"Elementary, my dear Watson!"

---

[10] Sir Arthur Conan Doyle, "The Dancing Men," in *The Return of Sherlock Holmes* (London: George Newnes, 1905).

---

[11] Sir Arthur Conan Doyle, "The Solitary Cyclist," in *The Return of Sherlock Holmes* (London: George Newnes, 1905).

---

[12] Sir Arthur Conan Doyle, *A Study in Scarlet* (Philadelphia: J. B. Lippincott, 1890).

"I say Holmes, do you think our good friend Dr. Stutman would also have been able to deduce the singular clue of the monogram?"

"I rather doubt it Watson. For although Dr. Stutman has a great deal of scientific knowledge, I fear that like you my dear fellow, he has very little imagination."

**"I DON'T THINK THIS WORK-OUT
IS WORKING!"**

II. WALK, DON'T WORKOUT

"Of all the exercises, walking is the best possible exercise known to man. Habituate yourself to walk far everyday without fatigue."

—Thomas Jefferson

"ARE WE FIT AND HEALTHY YET?"

REG HIDER

CHAPTER 4

IF YOU'RE FIT YOU'RE HEALTHY—RIGHT?— WRONG!

"I'M FIT, THEN I'M HEALTHY"— RIGHT?—WRONG!

Most people, especially your exercise enthusiasts, equate fitness with being healthy. Nothing could be further from the truth. You can be *physically fit* and in *poor health,* or you can be *healthy* and not *physically fit.*

Physical fitness by definition means that you have built up the capacity to do physical activity. For example, you can lift heavier weights than when you first started your weight-lifting program, or you can run faster and farther than you did when you first began your running program. In other words, physical fitness refers to the ability to do more physical activity with less effort than was required when you were "physically unfit." Now that you're physically fit, that means you're healthy, right? *Wrong!*

Being **healthy** means one thing only—to be *free of disease!* You can be the most physically fit man or woman in America and still be filled with cancer or arthritis or severe heart disease. Doesn't running or other strenuous exercise make the heart healthy? Definitely not! Doesn't jogging strengthen the arteries and the lungs? Not in a million years! So what's all this talk about running and jogging being so good for you? It's a bunch of baloney!

Strenuous exercises including jogging do nothing but condition and strengthen the muscles engaged in the actual exercise, in particular, the legs, arms, back, chest wall and respiratory muscles. These are the muscles that are getting the workout. These are the muscles that are getting the extra oxygen. These are the muscles that are hogging extra oxygen from all the other poor organs in the body that are not exercising. And when these gluttonous muscles can't get enough of everybody else's oxygen, they beg, borrow and steal and eventually go into **oxygen debt**.

Remember our little murder mystery about aerobic and anaerobic exercise? During **aerobic exercise** when the muscle pigs are slurping up all the oxygen they can get, the rest of the non-exercising organs (kidneys, gastrointestinal tract, etc.) get short-changed on their supply of oxygen. And during **anaerobic exercise** when the muscle hogs go into oxygen debt, the rest of the poor organs again have their blood supply diverted away so that they can't get enough oxygen. And finally, when the muscles are too pooped to pop, and they stop exercising so they can get enough oxygen to pay off this oxygen debt, the other poor starving organs must again wait their turn for the oxygen to reach their tiny cells. *Who said life was fair?*

You may have beautiful biceps, triceps and quadriceps, but you might have ugly sick kidneys, liver, spleen and gastrointestinal tract—not to mention your pancreas, adrenal glands, ovaries or testicles! So, remember that during and after strenuous exercise, the rest of the non-exercising parts of the body must patiently wait their turn for the oxygen rich blood to reach them. And if they have to wait too long, then, as we have previously seen, permanent irreversible damage may occur in the cells of these organs.

SURVIVAL OF THE FITTEST— NOT THE FASTEST!

A recent study from the University of Chicago indicated that experimental monkeys with slowed heart rates had 50% less cholesterol plaque build-up in their arteries than monkeys with faster heart rates. Both groups of monkeys were fed high-fat, high-cholesterol diets for 6 months. In spite of this diet, the monkeys with the slower heart rates were less susceptible to heart disease than those with the faster heart rates.

This study confirms previous reports that a regular lifetime walking program produces the fitness effect that leads to a slower resting pulse, which results in less heart disease. And remember, you don't have to speed up your heart rate in a walking program to attain physical fitness. No one has ever proved that a rapid heartbeat during strenuous exercise makes you healthy and fit.

On the contrary, here again is another study, proving that faster is not always better. The *faster the heart rate—the faster you get heart disease,* no matter what you eat. It makes sense! Your heart is not a mechanical motor that you can race all over the country. By racing it faster and faster, you don't make it run any better. In fact, the more you abuse your heart the faster it will give out on you. Don't forget, the heart can't stop beating overnight for rest and relaxation. It keeps on beating—we hope! Your heart is a delicate complex organ which must be **walked gently** every day, to keep it in proper working order.

PROTECT PREGNANT PATIENTS

The so-called fitness experts have been telling pregnant women for the past 10 years that exercise is beneficial for them. Magazines, videotapes and books have been giving the same message loud and clear— "it's okay to exercise when you're pregnant, you'll have a healthier baby."

Well, guess what? This advice is all wrong. Recent animal studies show that strenuous exercise during pregnancy may be potentially harmful to the fetus. This apparently happens because of two reasons. First, strenuous exercise may redirect the blood flow away from the uterus and placenta toward the mother's exercising muscles and skin. Any decrease in the blood's supply of oxygen to the developing fetus can be hazardous—causing birth defects, miscarriages, premature births and even fetal deaths.

Secondly, strenuous exercise causes an elevation of the body temperature in the pregnant woman. This rise in temperature is transmitted through the bloodstream to the fetus. This elevated temperature may cause damage to the fetus' developing nervous system resulting in neurologic birth defects. Recent studies in humans have verified these experimental animal studies.

Pregnancy itself makes greater demands on the cardiovascular and muscular system, so it stands to reason that physical exertion should be limited. Strenuous calisthenics, especially leg exercises, strain the ligaments supporting the uterus. And pregnancy causes a woman's center of gravity to shift, making a fall or injury more likely while exercising.

Always check with your own physician before embarking upon any exercise program, even walking. Most physicians, I'm sure would agree that walking is the safest, most beneficial form of exercise for the 1st half of your pregnancy. The fitness industry isn't concerned about your health. They are interested in one thing only—to make money selling equipment, apparel, books, video-cassettes, magazines and the rest of their snake-oil remedies. First have a baby that's healthy and serene. Then start walking to make your figure trim and lean.

MOM—"I FAILED FITNESS & FATNESS"

American children are less fit now than at any other time in the past 15 years. The President's Council on Physical Youth Fitness study has shown that young people's performance levels on various tests of physical endurance have steadily declined over the past 10-15 years. In addition, as many as 15% of children over the age of 12 had high blood pressure, 30% had high blood cholesterol and more than 40% were overweight. This trend increases the likelihood of heart attacks and other serious disorders in adulthood.

Part of the blame for America's unfit children comes from the lack of adequate physical education programs in the schools. The most important cause, however, is the life-style and eating habits of these children. The typical teenager spends an average of 3-5 hours a day watching TV and consuming large quantities of pre-packaged junk food. The only exercise that most teenagers get is walking to the car and driving over to a fast food restaurant for a burger and french fries.

Ask a typical teenager why he doesn't walk and he'll answer, "What for?" Nobody ever asked him to walk over to the store or walk to school. It isn't in his memory bank to walk anywhere except back and forth to the refrigerator or from one class to another in school. And most of today's kids will miss more than one-third of their gym classes with either a note from home or a medical excuse.

Get your little kids in the habit of walking everywhere. Let them see they have feet. Tell them the car is broken. Let them go out and play, really play—not just watch TV over a friend's house. Don't let them out of gym class every time they have the sniffles. And most important of all, let them see that you walk too. You can walk over to the store once in a while. One day just say, "Johnny, I'm going out for a walk." Maybe it will lay dormant somewhere in his memory bank and when he's older and wiser he'll call it up on his brain's screen and say, "boy, that's a neat idea."

PARENTS PROTECT PRECIOUS POSSESSIONS

Teenagers are among their parents' most prized possessions and should be protected from team sports. By this I mean that all prospective athletes should undergo a complete physical examination. This exam should include a detailed medical history along with any laboratory tests that their physician feels is indicated. They should have a careful evaluation of their blood pressure, pulse, heart sounds, heart rate and rhythm and pulses in their arms, legs and neck. Sometimes it is also necessary to take the blood pressure in the legs.

Any student or teenager who is found to have a heart murmur, an abnormal heart rhythm, any abnormal heart sounds or elevated blood pressure must have further studies before being allowed to participate in team sports. Those students also with a history of heart murmurs, abnormal heart rhythms, valvular heart disease, high blood pressure or vascular problems also need a complete cardiac workup.

The testing for these students must include an electrocardiogram, an echocardiogram, a stress EKG, a chest x-ray, a complete blood and urine analysis, and any other tests that the patient's physician may recommend.

Many unnecessary sports-related injuries and deaths could be avoided by this type of workup. No child or teenager should be engaging in competitive or team sports who has a heart or vascular problem, unless he gets a complete medical clearance from his physician. Too many tragic deaths occur every year because a student is playing sports with a potentially dangerous undiagnosed heart, vascular or medical problem.

TO BE FIT OR NOT TO BE

To be fit or not to be: that is the question! "Whether 'tis nobler in the mind to suffer the slings and arrows" of strenuous exercise, "or to take arms against a sea" of joggers, "and by opposing end them? To die; to sleep; no more; and by a sleep to say we end the heartache and the thousand natural shocks that flesh is heir to"—from the pounding feet and broken bones.

The question is not whether you should exercise or not, but actually what type of exercise is safe and beneficial. The answer is quite simply—*walking!* Walking is a safe, moderate intensity, rhythmic exercise, which provides all of the health, fitness and cardiovascular benefits of strenuous exercise, without the slings, arrows and other hazards.

Many fitness experts are now advocating a more moderate approach to exercise. Activities at home or at work may provide the same fitness and health benefits as a vigorous strenuous workout at the gym. Mowing the lawn, painting a room, working in the garden, or a simple walk around the block appear to provide the body with the same aerobic conditioning effects that were thought to be only the result of strenuous exercise.

In a recent study at the University of Minnesota's

School of Public Health, researchers found that moderate activities such as walking, home repair, gardening and other similar activities decreased the incidence of heart disease in middle-aged men. They also found that these activities seemed to also prevent further heart problems in men who already had coronary heart disease.

A study conducted at the University of Pittsburgh School of Medicine found that sedentary men who walked regularly showed a significant rise in the good cholesterol (HDL) in their blood. This HDL cholesterol appears to have a protective effect on the heart from developing heart disease. What was interesting about this study was that several different groups of men were exercised at varying levels of intensity for 20 minute periods. The HDL cholesterol levels rose just as much with low and moderate intensity walking as it did with the high intensity exercise periods. However, the most important finding was that the HDL cholesterol remained elevated longer in the walkers. *Walk, don't run,* and your HDL will stay up by gum.

In a 20 year study of 17,000 Harvard alumni, ages 35 to 74, a lifetime habit of moderate exercise was said to reduce heart attacks almost half as much as in those who were sedentary. In this study even smokers, or men who had high blood pressure or a history of heart disease, benefited from a regular program of exercise (Stanford Study, Dr. Ralph Paffenbarger, 1981). This report showed that an activity which burns approximately 300 to 350 calories daily resulted in a markedly decreased incidence of heart disease. Walking one hour every day burns approximately **350 calories** and has been shown to be the safest and most effective exercise for most people.

There is no evidence whatsoever that supports the theory that stressing the heart and vital organs with strenuous exercise strengthens them against stress. Most physicians are now recommending mild to moderate exercise for their patients. All of the medical evidence points to the fact that even mild exercise helps to prevent heart disease. Some exercise enthusiasts refuse to believe that exercise can be beneficial unless it is stressful, painful and exhausting. These die-hard individuals will go down for the count with disease, disability and death no matter what you tell them. *Walk, Don't Die* and let the exercise-nuts believe their lie.

AEROBICS NOT HEROICS

Exercise can be divided into two types—aerobic and anaerobic. *Aerobic exercises* include walking, swimming, tennis, cycling, running and other similar activities. Aerobic exercise improves both physical fitness and endurance and produces what is called cardiovascular conditioning. This is brought about by the repetitive action of large groups of muscles (legs, back, chest wall) which supplies a continuous supply of blood-rich oxygen to circulate through these muscles. Aerobic exercise also expends or burns fuel (calorie content of food). This type of exercise improves the efficiency of the cardiovascular, pulmonary and circulatory systems, and is considered to be a primary factor in the prevention of heart, lung and circulatory diseases.

Anaerobic exercises such as weight lifting, rapid or long distance running, or isometrics actually impair the flow of blood through these exercising muscles. This occurs because you are actually building up lactic acid in the muscles and increasing the peripheral resistance. When the blood flow to these muscles is impaired and lactic acid builds up, fatigue and pain in the muscles occurs, and the exercise must be stopped because of the lack of oxygen (oxygen debt). Anaerobic exercise may increase both the blood pressure and the heart rate by a reflex chemical and nervous system response to this impaired flow of blood through the muscles. This type of exercise can be potentially hazardous, especially for people with a history of high blood pressure, heart disease or vascular problems.

Walking is the ideal aerobic exercise to promote *cardiovascular fitness*. It should be done at least four times per week and you should walk for 30-60 minutes each day. While many earlier studies suggested that the heart rate during exercise should be 75-85% higher than the normal resting heart rate, more recent medical reports indicate that this is far in excess of what would seem to be a safe heart rate during exercise and may in fact be potentially dangerous. The so-called "target heart rate" is a fallacy and as we have previously stated, no one has ever proved that a rapid heart rate during exercise is in any way beneficial.

Walking at a comfortable rate of 3 mph will increase the heart rate 35-45% above the normal heart rate and this is more than sufficient to improve the lungs' and heart's ability to extract oxygen from the atmosphere and to increase its delivery to all the cells of the body. This cardiovascular conditioning process takes place over many months so that the body can adapt gradually to this increase in oxygen uptake and delivery.

Many medical studies have indicated that even though walking is a lower intensity activity than jogging, cardiovascular fitness appears to last longer in people who walk regularly as compared to those "flash in the pan" runners. With all the possible hazards of running—why run when you can walk. So it may take a little longer—better to be safe than sorry. *Slow and steady wins the fitness race.*

The following chart (Figure 1) illustrates the effects of walking on the physical fitness of middle-aged men between the ages of 40-57 years. By walking for 40 minutes four days a week, over a period of 20 weeks, these men showed a significant decrease in their resting heart rate, body weight, body fat and the time taken to walk a mile. They all also had a significant increase in their maximum oxygen uptake which is demonstrated in the first column.

FIGURE 1

Effects of walking on physical fitness of middle-aged men.

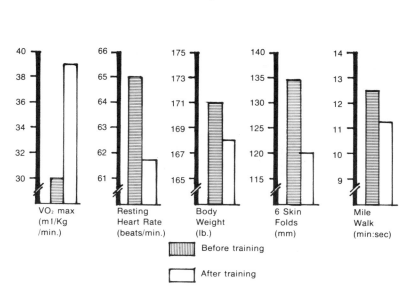

VO_2 max—Maximum oxygen uptake (aerobic capacity)
Body weight—determined by underwater weighing technique
Skin folds—Body fat determined by skin folds measurement

Reprinted with permission of The Physician and Sportsmedicine, *a McGraw-Hill publication, from an article "How Much Exercise is Enough?" by Michael L. Pollock, Ph.D., June 1978.*

WHAT THEN IS GOOD HEALTH?

As we have already stated, being fit is not necessarily being healthy. You can be in good health but be physically unfit or you can be in poor health and be physically fit. The best combination of course would be to be in good health and be physically fit also. Let's look at the ways we can obtain both fitness and good health.

I'll bet you are thinking, well of course he'll say walking is the answer. Right? Wrong again! No form of exercise whatsoever, even the best and safest exercise in the world—"walking"—can insure good health. It can help of course, but it can't do the entire job.

First of all you must get a complete physical examination every year from your physician. This examination may include blood tests, urinalysis, EKG, chest x-ray, breathing test, Pap smear, mammogram, prostate exam, examination for colon cancer, glaucoma and retinal exam, hearing tests and other studies that your physician thinks are indicated, as for example a stress EKG or an echocardiogram.

Secondly, when you are told that you have a medical condition you should follow your physician's instructions. For example, if you have to take blood pressure medication every day, take it! It's a small price to pay to prevent a stroke or heart attack.

Thirdly, never ignore any unusual medical symptoms or signs of illness. If you have a question, ask your doctor; don't wait until symptoms get worse.

And last but not least follow **the 24 good S's** and avoid the **2 dozen bad S's** for good health and a long life.

GOOD S's	BAD S's
1. Strolling & Walking daily	1. Sedentary life-style
2. Smile & Laughter	2. Stress
3. Sleep (6-8 hours)	3. Saturated Fat & Cholesterol
4. Seat Belts (wear them)	4. Spirits (alcohol)

5. Sex

5. Strenuous exercise

6. Solitude & Serenity

6. Smoking

7. Sky—get outdoors

7. Salt

8. Sand, sea & surf

8. Sugar

9. Skin care
(Sun blockers, etc.)

9. Sun—excess (Skin Cancer)

10. Safety caps on pills

10. Stimulants (caffeine,
diet pills, speed, etc.)

11. Song (music)

11. Sedatives (tranquilizers,
barbiturates, etc.)

12. Stationary bike

12. Sitting

13. Spiritual awareness

13. Sins—7 deadly

14. Stop, slow down and relax

14. Speeding while driving

15. Scriptures/Sabbath

15. Selfishness

16. Smoke detectors

16. Sadness and depression

17. Safety helmets
(bikes & sports)

17. Sadistic behavior

18. Sports (walking, golf,
swimming, bowling,
tennis—doubles only)

18. Sports (jogging, racketball, weight lifting,
strenuous calisthenics)

19. Shoes
(good pair for walking)

19. Self-pity

20. Success—strive for

20. Self-righteousness

21. Sincerity & sympathy

21. Smugness and snobishness

22. Self-confidence &
Self-awareness

22. Sullen and sour disposition

23. Steam cooking (preserves
freshness & nutrients)

23. Smoked meats & fishes
(contain cancer-
causing nitrites)

24. **S-Good Foods** (salads—
vegetable & fruit; soups
(not creamed); sandwich
bread (whole grain); skim
milk & non-fat dairy
products; spaghetti &
pasta; squash, stringbeans
& other vegetables;
strawberries and other
fruits; seafood—salmon,
swordfish, scrod, sea trout,
sea bass, snapper)

24. **S-Bad Foods** (salad
dressings; sauces; sauteed
foods; sweets & syrups; sour
cream & saturated fat dairy
products—eggs, whole
milk, cheese, butter; salt-
cured and pickled foods;
steak and meats; salami &
lunchmeats; shellfish—
shrimp, scallops, lobster
and crab)

—SEE CHAPTER 7 FOR ALL THE FABULOUS F-FOODS—

"I GUESS THIS IS THE RIGHT WAY TO USE
THIS MACHINE BECAUSE THE PAIN
IS KILLING ME!"

CHAPTER 5

CRIPPLING CALISTHENICS & THE MANGLE MACHINES

MASS MASOCHISM

Americans follow, for all intents and purposes, the pain-pleasure principle. In order for an activity, exercise, or diet to be good for you, it must hurt first, and if it is easy, it certainly can't be beneficial. In other words, we follow the punishment-reward principle. If you follow a strict diet, that will lead to a thin, trim body. Or if we engage in strenuous, back-breaking exercises, then, of course, we will become fit and trim. How many of you have sat at the beach or at a pool and encountered a painful sunburn in order to have a beautiful summer tan.

The diets that we follow usually are aimed at fast results, so we look for the fast gimmick or fad diet in order to lose weight rapidly. Other extremes can be seen in the health food and vitamin industry. If a certain amount of a vitamin or mineral is listed as the correct dosage for good health, we then assume that larger amounts must be better.

And finally we come to the exercise-fitness mania which has become a major industry overnight in America. We have gone from a sedentary existence to marathon-type exercises and have overlooked the simpler, more moderate forms of exercise. If it's flashy and aerobic, it must be good. Not since the days of the Roman gladiators has a population engaged in such dangerous sports. Injuries and deaths by the thousands have resulted from these *awful aerobic acrobatics*. Mass masochism had overtaken America—*"if it hurts bad, it must be good"*!

WORKOUTS WEAKEN

One of the biggest hoaxes to be perpetrated on the American public in the last 10 years is that strenuous exercises like jogging, back-breaking calisthenics and heavy exercise machines, make your heart and arteries stronger. That's just ridiculous! The only thing strenuous exercise does is to build up and strengthen the exercising muscles themselves—in particular the leg, arm, chest wall and respiratory muscles. This results from the increased consumption of oxygen by these exercising muscles.

The heart and arteries don't benefit at all by this type of exercise, and, in fact, they may have trouble getting enough oxygen during strenuous exercise. Ordinarily there is a built-in protective mechanism that regulates the amount of oxygen the heart muscle extracts from the bloodstream. This is relatively constant no matter how fast your heart beats. If we are sitting still or walking fast, the heart still extracts its regular supply of oxygen from the blood carried by the coronary arteries.

What happens then when we start to pretend we're super-men and women? The amount of oxygen needed by the exercising parts of the body (arms, legs, chest and respiratory muscles) begins to dramatically increase. To supply this extra oxygen, the heart must beat faster and faster in order to pump a greater volume of blood to provide this additional oxygen.

Now, in order to pump this larger volume of blood at an even faster rate, the heart begins to cry out—"I need more oxygen too, if you want me to keep up this ridiculous pace." So the coronary arteries have to carry more blood to the heart, so it can get enough oxygen, to have enough strength, to pump more blood to those crazy exercising muscles. Now that's what I call sheer lunacy.

Who ever said that the faster our hearts go, the more fit we are? Some physicial fitness nut probably thought that up in the back of a sweaty gym. And, lo and behold, another fitness myth was created—that you have to get your *"target heart rate"* up to 70-80 percent of maximum. Maximum what? *Maximum death probably!*

And now for the punch line, if you're not already punchy enough from all this cow manure about getting a stronger heart from strenuous exercise. Remember we said that the heart had to beat faster and faster, in order to pump enough blood for those wild and crazy muscle guys. And remember we realized that in order to keep up this frantic pace, the heart needed to gulp down more oxygen just to stay ahead of the game. Well, what do you think happens to the poor fellow who has narrowed coronary arteries and doesn't know it. His heart just can't get enough oxygen during these strenuous exercises, because his arteries are too narrow to carry enough blood to the heart. Not enough blood—not enough oxygen and—bingo—a **heart attack** or **sudden cardiac death**!

This poor guy would probably have lived another

20 years if he hadn't thought that these false idols—
jogging, strenuous calisthenics and weight lifting—
would prolong his life. He probably wouldn't even have
had any heart symptoms for another 10 years unless
he over-stressed his heart. And he probably would
have been to a doctor a lot sooner for a check-up, if he
hadn't bought the American myth that anyone in
America can be anything he wants to be, including old,
if he works hard, plays hard and runs faster than the
next guy. This poor chump not only bought the Brook-
lyn Bridge, he bought the farm!

CALISTHENICS CRIPPLE

One out of every two people who engage in aerobic
exercises are injured. In a study of over 1,500 aerobic
students, more than 700 of them reported injuries
ranging from simple shin splints to fractured bones
and slipped discs. Contrary to popular belief, the more
frequently you exercised, the chances of injury increased significantly.

These injuries were thought to be caused by over-
exercise, improper shoes, and hard, non-resilient floor
surfaces. However, injuries occurred in many individuals who took proper precautions. The fact of the matter is that there is no medical benefit to jumping up
and down whether the floor is hard or soft, or whether
you are wearing the correct shoes. Aside from stretching your muscles, which incidentally is completely
worthless as an exercise, you are doing nothing to
improve your level of fitness.

Calisthenics and aerobic dancing are social functions, not fitness builders. Yes, to some extent you are
increasing the maximum oxygen consumption, but
only for short spurts which produces no lasting cardiovascular benefits. Remember, no one has ever proved
that getting your heart rate up to astronomical numbers for short periods of time improves your level of

cardiovascular fitness. On the contrary, most recent medical studies indicate that this rapid pulse rate theory may actually be potentially hazardous to your health.

Calisthenics cripple by breaking bones, pulling muscles, stretching ligaments, and ripping tendons. **Aerobic dancing damages** feet, ankles, knees, hips and spines by pneumatic-drill type bouncing. **Weight machines mangle** by straining ligaments, ripping muscles, tearing tendons and bulging biceps. Many of these musculo-skeletal injuries cause temporary damage; others result in permanent disability. As far as I'm concerned aerobics are awful and calisthenics are crazy.

Well you're saying, what's so bad about a few pulled muscles or torn tendons? Wait! I haven't finished yet with the more serious complications of these crippling calisthenics. *Irregular heartbeats* are common among both men and women who engage in aerobic classes. They are caused by the extreme stress of the exercise and an unconditioned cardiovascular system. In most cases they are not harmful. However, in many cases they are potentially dangerous, leading to more serious heartbeat irregularities, heart attacks, and even sudden death.

Many people who start aerobic classes and think they are in good health may have *underlying congenital or acquired heart abnormalities* that they are completely unaware of. They may have had a heart murmur as a child and were told that it would probably go away when they got older. Many relatively minor heart conditions in childhood have remained undiagnosed because of the lack of accurate diagnostic tests 20-30 years ago, and because these people have never had any symptoms of heart disease. They feel fine, have no chest pain or palpitations and are leading perfectly normal lives—until they start these crippling calisthenics. Then they may develop chest pain, shortness of breath, marked fatigue or palpitations. Often it is attributed to "just being out of shape" and these aerobic robots continue on their casualty-course toward disability and death.

One such common congenital heart condition with usually no symptoms whatsoever, called *mitral valve prolapse* (MVP), is being discovered with increased frequency today, primarily in women. The advent of a test known as the echocardiogram has now made this condition easy to diagnose. However, many women who join aerobic classes and are unaware of this heart condition, are at considerable risk when they strenuously exercise. The mitral valve is actually a one way opening between two chambers of the heart. Mitral valve prolapse is actually a floppy valve which may cause some of the blood to leak back into the heart chamber where it came from. In most cases it is a completely benign condition causing no symptoms whatsoever. But in strenuous exercise it may cause more blood to leak backwards and interfere with the heart's ability to pump blood. It may start to become apparent by just a few "skipped heartbeats" or it may evolve into a dangerous irregular heart rhythm. How many aerobic classes give *free EKG's and echocardiagrams* to new members?

How about our typical overweight middle-aged male with underlying, *undiagnosed coronary heart disease* or *hypertension*. He has no symptoms, joins the awful acrobatic aerobics class, starts his crazy calisthenics and drops dead. He probably had some chest pain and shortness of breath when he started his jumping jacks aerobics class. But he just ignored it and thought he too was "just out of shape" like the rest of his overweight classmates. And he certainly wasn't going to stop in the middle of his exercise class while the rest of the aerobic robots, including the 21-year-old athletic instructor, were effortlessly jumping and stumping. So he just exercised on through his pain and strain and kept on "looking good" as they wheeled him out on the stretcher. How many fitness clubs offer *free stress EKG's and coronary arteriograms* along with their membership fees?

Walk Don't Run and live to have fun. Leave the calisthenics for the crazies, the weight machines for the maniacs, and the aerobics classes for the acrobatic asses. *Walk, Don't Die,* let the aerobic acrobats fly.

HEALTH CLUBS ARE A PAIN IN THE GLUTEUS MAXIMUS

Most health clubs are usually located some distance from your home or work, thus you have to spend time traveling. Even those located fairly close to you still involve driving and parking, and then driving and parking again back home or to the office.

What about gym clothes? Well, there's your gym bag and perhaps a locker. How many times have you thought that you left gym clothes in your locker (if you have one) or in your car and arrived ready for your workout and found you had no shoes or shorts—another missed exercise session.

Or if you arrive at the health club before work or during lunchtime and find there's not enough time for a shower, how long do you think that double dose of antiperspirant will work at work? Not long enough! Have you ever also noticed that your car takes on the aroma of your dirty gym clothes after they've remained there for awhile? Just look at the funny expressions on your friends' faces when you give them a ride.

Well, you finally decide to wait until after work to go to the health club, that way your co-workers can get a break. So what happens? Between 5-6 PM the pool is so crowded that you can't dip your toe in. The line for the exercise machines is backed up half way around the gym. And the exercise bikes are reserved until 10 PM. So you go over to the aerobic exercise class only to find out you that you just missed the 6 PM session and that the next session is for advanced karate experts only.

The only workout you got was getting into and out of your sweatsuit. You go over to the manager to complain and he tells you that it's never crowded at 6 AM or 11 PM at night. And try to get even part of your membership fee back. Forget it!

DANGEROUS DANCING

Aerobic dancing may be good for the waistline but it's bad for the back and legs. In a recent study reported in The Physician and Sportsmedicine Journal, injuries occurred in over half of the women who participated in aerobic dance classes. In a related study almost 75 percent of participants suffered some form of injury.

The most common injuries were:
1. **Shin splints** (injuries to the ligaments over the shin bone with resultant pain when walking)
2. **Ankle injuries** (ligament tears) and pulled calf muscles
3. **Sprain of the Achilles' tendon** in back of ankle
4. **Stress fractures** of the small bones of the feet
5. **Lower back injuries** ranging from pulled back muscles and torn ligaments to slipped discs

These injuries were caused primarily because of wearing no shoes or shoes without adequate support. Hard floors and excessive dancing were also reported to contribute to injuries. And lastly, most women who engaged in aerobic dancing were not sufficiently conditioned to take the excessive strain put on their ligaments, muscles and joints. Once these joints and ligaments are injured, the re-injury rate almost doubles because of inadequate healing time given for recovery in most cases.

Why do a *dangerous dance* when you can take a

wonderful walk with all the same health and fitness benefits, and without the hazards and dangers. **Walk, don't limp!**

I DON'T LIKE THOSE ODDS!

In a recent study in <u>The New England Journal of Medicine</u>, it was reported that vigorous, strenuous exercise helps to protect people from sudden heart attacks even though the odds of having a heart attack are higher during the work-out than at other times. Well, "excuse me"! Those odds are lousy. It sounds like the ones who survive the work-out are the only ones that live longer. You have a better chance playing Russian roulette.

The study found that men who exercise regularly have a lower than normal risk of having a heart attack only at times when they are not vigorously exercising. However, during their work-out they are more likely than usual to suffer a cardiac arrest. This study was trying to show that strenuous exercise is more help than harm. It sure doesn't sound like that to me!

I'll stick to walking, where the risk of having a heart attack with or without cardiac arrest is much lower before walking, while walking and after walking! Even if there's the slightest doubt, **Walk, Don't Workout.** The best odds you can buy are to **Walk, Don't Die**.

THE MANGLE MACHINES

There are many types of indoor exercise mangle machines that can be found at your expensive health club. Most of these are extremely dangerous and difficult to use. Muscle injuries, ligament tears, tendon ruptures, back and neck muscle spasms are but a few of the many treats in store for you when you *tangle with the mangle machines.*

1. **MULTI-PURPOSE GYM MUSCLE MACHINES:** These include the so-called new ball-bearing weight-stack-lifting machines and various springs, cables, pulleys, and elastic stretching devices. This type of exercise stresses the stimulation and strengthening of the large muscles of the body. These machines do very little for the heart and lung capacity and do not increase the consumption of oxygen; therefore, they are not useful in fitness conditioning, nor in burning calories to help you to lose weight. Many of these muscle gym machines can be dangerous and have been known to cause elevation of blood pressure in susceptible persons. Fitness centers lead you to believe that because these weight-stack machines are on ball-bearings, they are safe to use. That's sheer nonsense. Weight lifting with weight-machines has the same dangers as free weights.

2. **ANKLE AND WRIST WEIGHTS:** Whoever thought of exercising or doing calisthenics with weights on your ankles and wrists should have weights tied to his hands and feet and be dropped in the ocean. There is enough strain on the heart during exercise without making it more hazardous to your health. Remember, exercise doesn't have to be painful for it to be beneficial.

3. **SIT BACK AND DO NOTHING MACHINES** (Belt Vibrators, Roller Machines, and Whirlpool Baths): These so-called exercise devices contribute absolutely nothing towards the development of cardiovascular fitness. They are not aerobic exercise or any other exercise for that matter, and are potentially dangerous. Roller machines can cause small blood vessels to break under the skin causing hemorrhages. Belt vibrators have been implicated in jarring internal abdominal organs with occasional damage to these vital structures.

4. **BARBELLS, DUMBBELLS, AND OTHER HEAVY FREE WEIGHTS:** All are dangerous and can cause back, arm, leg, and hip injuries. Some people have developed hernias from weight lifting. Heavy weights may aggravate or cause high blood pressure in some people. Barbells are for dumbbells.

5. **MINI-TRAMP:** These miniature trampolines are often called rebounders. They are three or four feet wide and are approximately 4-8 inches off the ground. There are many injuries reported with these rebounders. They include falls from loss of balance, ankle and knee sprains from twisting, head and neck injuries from bouncing too high and hitting an overhang, and back and hip injuries from twisting.

6. **ROWING MACHINES:** This particular mangle machine is really designed to develop upper body strength, not cardiovascular fitness. These machines also can be dangerous to people with high blood pressure or heart disease because they can actually raise the blood pressure. They can also cause a variety of back problems ranging from pulled muscles to slipped discs.

7. **TREADMILL:** The treadmill is actually a conveyor belt supported by a steel frame. They come in both motorized and non-motorized varieties and both are extremely dangerous to use. They put excessive strain on the back and leg muscles, causing a variety of injuries ranging from simple muscle and ligament sprains to more severe back injuries.

8. **INDOOR SKI TRACK MACHINES:** The newest and perhaps most dangerous entry into the home exercise market is the indoor ski track machine. These contraptions supposedly simulate cross country skiing in your living room. You hook your feet into two wooden ski-like contraptions which slide back and forth as you move your legs forward and backward. Then you grab on to two pulleys with

each arm and attempt to pull them simultaneously as you slide back and forth on the wooden slats. The only problem is that you have to pull the pulley with the arm opposite to the leg that is moving forward? Sound easy? Forget it. Even if you've skied before, unless you are a contortionist, this complicated apparatus is for the birds. Reports of fractured leg bones, torn arm muscles and broken hips are but a few of the reported injuries related to the use of these new mangle machines.

SEE JACK SWEAT

The newest exercise craze to hit the rich and famous are the so-called "personal fitness trainers." For $100-$250 an hour you can strain and sweat under the watchful eye of your very own exercise guru. These trainers will come to your home or office and supervise your exercise work-out. They make sure that you sweat the correct number of liters per hour and they measure your biceps and quadriceps muscles with gold-lamé measuring tapes.

These disco ducks are the ultimate rip-offs in the fast-growing health and fitness industry. These so-called experts are not required to be licensed and there is no quality control in who chooses to call himself a "personal trainer." There may be a few qualified people out there who have been trained in exercise physiology. But, in general, this is another big scam perpetuated on the rich and not-so-rich Americans, seeking the elusive bird of fitness. You can become your own personal trainer by telling yourself "don't talk, just take a walk."

STEROID SUICIDE

One of the newer drugs to be used with hazardous results are the so called **"anabolic steroids."** These steroids (male hormones) are being used with increasing frequency to build muscle mass in athletics. This steroid abuse has resulted in very serious side effects, ranging from heart disease, immune system failure, liver disease including liver cancer, hypertension and mental disorders.

Many women who are **"into body building"** have tried these anabolic steroids with hazardous results. They began to develop facial hair, the voice deepens, menstrual cycles become abnormal, and the breasts begin to shrink. Many of these changes can be permanent even if women try to counteract them with female hormones. These steroids have also caused irreversible damage to the ovaries, making reproduction impossible. We will soon have an army of barren body-builders to send into battle.

CALISTHENICS CONFUSE CORPORATIONS

Consumer sales of exercise and fitness equipment will exceed $1 billion this year and are predicted to top $2.5 billion by 1990. According to the President's Council on Physical Fitness, corporations offering employee fitness programs have increased from a few hundred in 1973 to well over 5,000 today. The Association for Fitness in Business which was founded in 1974 with 25 members has grown to more than 3,000.

American corporations are actually confused about calisthenics. They could save all that money and pass it on as bonuses to their employees, if they understood the first basic law of exercise physiology. Exercise doesn't have to be painful or stressful to be beneficial. You don't need fancy exercise equipment or corporate health clubs. Walking provides all the same health, fitness and weight-control benefits as all the other strenuous calisthenics and exercises put together. Give any employee a ½ hour break to go out for a walk and you'll get a refreshed, productive, happy person.

THE WEAKENED, WEEK-END WARRIOR!

In a recent symposium at Rutgers Medical School, Dr. Aapo Lehonen, a lecturer in medicine at Finland's University of Turku, stated that moderate exercise has been proven to increase the good cholesterol (HDL) in the blood. **HDL cholesterol** has been noted to have a protective mechanism against the development of heart disease. Moderate aerobic exercise, according to Dr. Lehonen, seems to have the greatest effect on raising the HDL cholesterol, and, therefore, the most beneficial effect on the blood fats.

Aerobic exercise is defined as the type of exercise in which the oxygen demand of the large muscles of the body does not exceed the oxygen supply. This type of aerobic exercise usually occurs in constant, sustained exercise such as walking, but not in strenuous high-intensity exercises where the oxygen demand exceeds the oxygen supply.

Jogging and other strenuous exercises result in anaerobic metabolism, in which the oxygen demand is greater than the oxygen supply, resulting in a condition known as oxygen debt. Since the body has to spend all of its time trying to pay off this oxygen debt, it has no time or energy to sustain a high level of HDL cholesterol. Consequently, the protective effect on the heart is lost during these brief bursts of high-intensity activity.

The 9-5 desk worker who dashes on to the tennis or racketball courts each weekend is wasting his time and maybe his life. The weary business executive who gets up at dawn to jog or run every Saturday and Sunday morning should have stayed in bed, for all the good his exercise is doing him. These *week-end warriors are actually weakened,* not strengthened.

CHAPTER 6

"NO PAIN, NO GAIN"—THAT'S INSANE!

Millions of Americans who have joined fitness clubs in the past 10 years have been brain-washed by their so-called fitness instructors into believing the *"no pain, no gain"* fallacy. They have been intimidated into exercising "until it hurts," or when at the point of total exhaustion their instructor says—"do 5 more good ones." And if you want to look fit and trim like the 24 year old fitness instructor, you'd better "use it or lose it."

Well guess what? You've been handed another load of fertilizer. In a recent survey of over 1500 aerobic class participants, over 53% sustained injuries. These injuries included pulled muscles, sprained ligaments, stress fractures, dislocated joints, torn cartilages and slipped discs. Several cases of stress induced heart attacks and strokes were included among the list of injuries.

Most of these so-called fitness centers are run by instructors who've had no training at all in exercise physiology. Less than 10% of fitness instructors have degrees in exercise physiology or have been accredited by the American College of Sports Medicine. Many fitness clubs display a sign reading "our fitness instructors are certified." This probably means that the instructor attended a 2-day class to receive an exercise fitness certificate.

Most of these crazy calisthenic clubs don't even bother to take a medical history from their members. As long as you pay your dues up front, they could care less what happens to you! The fanatical fitness instructor freaks who run these side shows, think that everyone regardless of age, weight, sex or body build should be able to keep up with their continuous aerobic acrobatics. And when the first casualty occurs, and someone cries—"Who knows CPR?"—Who do you think is the first one out the door? You guessed it—our muscle bound fitness instructor.

> Save your money and save your time
> Fitness clubs are a pain in the behind
> If all you want is fitness and pep
> Then take a walk with a vigorous step
> These health clubs say "no pain, no gain"
> That's not only false, but that's insane

WALKING! NOW WHY DIDN'T I THINK OF THAT?

Of all the mysteries that have appeared over the centuries, one of the most difficult problems, second only to the solution of Egyptian hieroglyphics, has been the quest for the ultimate, easy, lifelong diet and fitness plan. The answer has lain dormant for all of eternity, yet has been visibly present all along like Poe's Purloined Letter—**WALKING!**

Walking has only just gained public attention and acclaim as an after-thought or alternative to the last popular American craze of jogging, which hit its peak in the 1970's. The jogging craze started on its decline in the early 1980's after hundreds of thousands of Americans succumbed to disabilities, injuries, and deaths resulting from this wild, barbaric, gladiator event. America then began to rediscover the ancient art of **WALKING**.

Each scientific specialist and researcher has claimed the discovery as his own, as if it were an ancient archaeological find of the most magnificent caliber.

The **physiologists** suddenly noted that walking offers the same benefits as jogging without the hazards.

The **orthopedic surgeons** quickly realized that walking has the same advantages as jogging without the fractures or dislocations. "Oh my aching wallet!"

A **cardiologist** stated emphatically, "Now I have an exercise to help my patients rehabilitate after a heart attack—walk for your heart."

"Alas," said the **surgeon**. "The diseases of arteries and veins, aided by this little-known remedy, will have to be kept secret or else I will have to drive an economy chariot."

"Forsooth," said the **foot doctor**. "I was just starting to make a go of it, with all those foot injuries. Maybe we can stamp out this discovery."

"Foiled again," said the **sports medicine physician**. "We've just created an entire specialty devoted to jogging injuries, which will go down the drain unless we muzzle this discovery. Who do we know in Washington?"

"My goodness," said the **bio-chemist**. "An ancient ritual to help the body distribute and utilize oxygen without the use of chemical additives—amazing!"

"Look out!" said the owner of an **exercise club**. "If this leaks out, we're finished! An exercise that works without stress or strain, sweat or pain—and no dues— we better check our rental agreement in this shopping center."

"Oh my God," said the **weight-loss center manager**—"If this gets out, we're done for. No one will spend money on our gimmicks if they can do it safely and effectively for nothing."

"That's the end of my business career," said the **diet doctor**. "If this gets around, I'll have to go back to being a doctor, and I think my license has already expired."

"Oh, no," said the **diet and fitness book authors**—"Now there will be nothing to write about. I wonder what's hot in yoga or maybe acupuncture?"

WALKERS GET NO RESPECT!

Although over 100 million Americans list walking as their number one form of exercise, walking still remains the stepchild of the fitness revolution. There isn't enough glamour or pizzazz in walking to make it a contender as a major exercise in the physical fitness movement.

What we need is a *show-biz celebrity* to come out with a line of walking clothes with a designer emblem certified by the <u>American National Health Council on Walking</u>, which incidentally, isn't in existence yet. Then we need a line of expensive monogrammed walking shoes which start at $75.00 and up, to show the world that we're walkers.

Next, we need a line of *walking accessories*. The old fashioned walking-stick made out of aged oak with carved ivory handles may be just the thing to get the walking movement started. In fact, a whole line of designer walking-sticks could serve double duty as a high-fashion conversation piece and as a weapon to ward off muggers. Monogrammed T-shirts, shorts, socks, headbands and sweatsuits all would increase the public's awareness of walking as a major sport. Even a "walking supporter" and a "walking bra" would do much to gain respectability for the walkers of America.

Now we need a few famous *celebrity athletes* to do a TV beer commercial extolling the benefits of walking and the need for a cold brew after their walking workout. Or a TV walking golf tournament sponsored by a major golf cart company showing the hazards of the electric golf cart in favor of the old fashioned walking golf cart.

Next, we'll need some major *walking marathons* sponsored by the companies that produce the latest high-fashion line of walking clothes and shoes. This will invariably lead to famous walkers revealing their innermost feelings about the euphoria that walking provides them with. And, of course, no respectable sport can be left out of the videocassette market. You'll be able to roll out of bed each morning and "walk-a-long" with Chuck or Babette in their bikini walking suits.

And let's not leave out the most important status symbol of the exercise revolution—*"injuries."* What respectable sport that's worth its salt doesn't have any injuries? Walkers will have to keep the fact that walking is virtually injury-free to themselves. They'll tell about how they "hit-rig" during their last walk, or how they walked 3 miles with a pebble in their shoe. A new line of injuries will be labeled—"walker's shin-splints", "Achilles walkingitis", "walker's wrath", "weary walker", "walker's wrench", "weakened walker", "walker's wrinkles", and so on and so forth. The field of sports-medicine will now have a new field of injuries to contend with and will be able to again make the TV talk show rounds discussing the various treatments for the wanton walkers of America.

But walking won't get the respect it deserves until the day comes when you can drive to your local walking health club, change into your designer walking clothes, walk a few laps on the indoor walking track, shower, change back into your street clothes and drive back home. And don't forget the dues. *Any fitness sport that has dues gets respect!*

WALKING'S WITCHCRAFT

There is considerable agreement among most exercise physiologists that exercise on a moderate, even basis has a tranquilizing effect. A rhythmic exercise like walking for 20-30 minutes, seems to be the most effective method for producing this tranquilizing effect.

Several theories have been proposed to explain this tranquilizing effect. One current theory is that a slight increase in body temperature affects the brain-stem and results in a rhythmic electrical activity in the cortex of the brain. This produces a more relaxed state and is the direct result of exercise. Other studies indicate that there is an increase in brain chemicals, particularly a group of chemicals called the endorphins. These appear to have a tranquilizing or sedative effect and result in relaxation.

In a recent study from Massachusetts General Hospital, reported in the New England Journal of Medicine, researchers suggested that regular exercise may increase the secretion of two chemicals called beta-endorphin and beta-lipotropin. These substances act as chemical pain killers or tranquilizers and thus can influence the body's metabolism and give a sense of tranquility and well being. This study noted that with exercise these levels of chemicals increased, and with more strenuous exercise this increase was even greater. This may, in part, explain the "runners' high" or "joggers' euphoria" that is reported with high-intensity exercise. They stated that this also may explain the withdrawal effect noted by runners after they stopped their running program and the frequency with which joggers sustain fractured bones while running without feeling any pain.

Walking, on the other hand, produces only a moderate rise in these brain chemicals. This results in a relaxed state of mind and produces a tranquilizing effect on the entire nervous system. Since walking is not a strenuous exercise, the level of these brain chemicals does not go too high, thus avoiding the analgesic or pain-killing effect produced with high-intensity exercises. This enables the walker to be aware of pain if he turns his ankle or foot while walking. The runner, on the other hand, because of the high analgesic levels of these brain chemicals, may not actually feel the chest pain from a heart attack and he may drop over dead before he becomes aware of the pain. The abnormally high levels of these brain chemicals in this case is another example of too much of a good thing—the devil's deadly death draught.

Walking's witchcraft, on the other hand, is just the magic you need to fight the devil's sorcery and the voodoo of everyday stress and tension. The calm, serene enchantment of walking (moderate levels of the tranquilizing brain chemicals), fights off the black-arts of tension, nervousness, anxiety and stress. Let the wonderful wizard of walking lead you down the peaceful path of restful relaxation. Now that's what I call a mouthful of tranquilizers!

THEY CAN'T FOOL ALL OF US ALL OF THE TIME

According to the latest Roper Poll October 1985, 50% of the United States population stated that walking was their favorite form of exercise. Surprised? Don't be. The fitness industry would like us to think otherwise. That's why hundreds of millions of dollars are spent each year on advertising health and fitness clubs, jogging apparel, aerobic centers, fitness machines and any other gimmicks that these advertisers can use to empty your wallets. Well take heart America, they can fool some of the people some of the time, but not all of the people all of the time. They won't advertise walking because they can't make a dime from it.

THE PERCENT OF ADULTS
WHO REGULARLY ENGAGE
IN VARIOUS FORMS OF EXERCISE

WALKING	————————————————	50%
CALISTHENICS	————————	19%
SWIMMING	————————	18%
BICYCLING	————————	16%
GOLF	————————	15%
TENNIS + RACKET-BALL	————————	14%
JOGGING	——————	10%
BOWLING	——————	9%

TAKE A HAPPY WALK

Americans are walking again like never before. According to the President's 1985 Council on Physical Fitness report, walking is the single most popular adult exercise in America. With over 44 million adherents, the numbers are steadily increasing as people of all ages are walking for health, fitness and fun. Walking is an exercise whose time has finally come. Why not? It's easy, safe, fun and it makes you feel and look great.

Walking is something that two people, no matter how different their physical condition, can do together. It is companionable exercise where you can enjoy each other's company and at the same time get all the benefits of exercising.

Walking is a great escape. You can get away from the phone, from the office, or from home for a little while and take that needed time to relax. You can walk to think out a problem or walk to forget one. Walking acts as a tranquilizer to help us relax and it can work as a stimulant to give us energy. The late famous cardiologist Dr. Paul Dudley White said that "A vigorous 5 mile walk will do more good for an unhappy but otherwise healthy adult than all the medicine and psychology in the world."

TAKE THAT STEP-UP TO SUCCESS

Don't make the common mistake of thinking that walking is too easy to be a good exercise. On the contrary, walking is not only the safest but it's the best exercise in the world. If you're overweight then walking is your best choice since you won't be putting excess stress on the ligaments, muscles, and joints.

How you walk also tells whether you're happy, sad, angry, ambitious or just plain lazy. Walkers with a long stride, a greater arm swing and a bounce to their step were happy, ambitious and self-assured whereas walkers with a short stride, a foot shuffle or drag and a short arm swing were often depressed, unhappy and angry.

Recent studies in women indicate that arm swing is the most indicative factor of their mood. The greater the arm swing the happier, more vigorous and less depressed the woman was. A short arm swing indicated that the woman was angry, frustrated and unhappy.

Stretch out your stride, swing your arm, and put a bounce in your step whenever and wherever you walk. That's your road to good health, a successful career and a long happy life. Believe it! It works!

HOW ABOUT A WALK
JUST FOR FUN!

Walk whenever you can, instead of driving. If you have to drive, park somewhere a few blocks from your destination and walk the difference. Take the stairs instead of the elevator whenever possible. Take a walk when you are in a new part of town or at a friend's home. Always walk when you are away from home to see the beauty of different surroundings. Enjoy your walk by exploring different areas around your home or office.

If the weather is bad you can go to an enclosed shopping mall and walk. You can stop and look in all the windows after you've completed your regular workout walk in the mall.

You don't have to time your pulse. You don't have to do warm up stretching exercises before you walk. You don't have to do cool down exercises when you finish. You don't have to tire yourself or get overheated or out of breath. You don't need special clothing or equipment, just a good pair of comfortable walking shoes. You don't have to be an athlete or an acrobat. All you have to do is walk your feet for fun and you automatically, without trying, will stay fit and trim.

WALK TO WORK AND CARRY YOUR LUNCH

According to a recent report from the Census Bureau many Americans still walk to work and many even carry their lunch. Thirty years ago, more than three times the number of people walked to work. However, with today's increased ease of transportation most Americans have given up this safe easy way to stay in shape. Let's give a hand to the 12 states that haven't given in to today's ride-everywhere society.

STATES WITH THE HIGHEST PERCENTAGE OF PEOPLE WALKING TO WORK

(Rounded off to nearest decimal point)

ALASKA	17.2%
NORTH DAKOTA	15.1%
MONTANA	14.6%
SOUTH DAKOTA	12.8%
WASHINGTON, D.C.	12.1%
VERMONT	11.4%
IOWA	9.5%
MAINE	9.3%
NEW YORK	8.7%
MASSACHUSETTS	7.8%
PENNSYLVANIA	7.6%
ILLINOIS	6.9%

"NO PAIN, MUCH GAIN— NOW THAT'S SANE!

If you are overweight or just have let yourself get out of shape, then you must feel as if you'd better start some form of exercise. Most of us are not very athletic and the thought of putting on jogging clothes or tights to do aerobics seems to put fear in the hearts of the bravest among us. Well, don't despair! You're not alone. There is an exercise that we can all do safely without fear. Yes, walking will keep you lean and serene.

Walking is a surreptitious way of exercising without making a spectacle of yourself. No need to put on special shoes or clothing. No need to join an expensive fitness club. No need to take time from work or home to drive to your exercise class. Just open up your front door and take a walk. Not just today, but everyday. Do it anytime you want to and walk wherever you want to go.

Walking is about the best overall exercise there is and it achieves the same fitness, health and weight control benefits as the other more hazardous exercises. Walking tones the muscles in your legs, hips, abdomen, chest and arms. Walking improves the efficiency of your cardiovascular system and it conditions the lungs to extract oxygen from the atmosphere more efficiently. Walking is one of the best ways to burn calories, helping you to lose and control weight more effectively.

Sounds too good to be true, doesn't it? Well it is. And what's more there are no injuries associated with walking. How about that? No runner's knee, no foot problems, no pulled muscles or torn ligaments, no broken bones and no injuries whatsoever.

And guess what else? It's not painful, stressful or tiring. So now you're asking, "if it doesn't hurt how can it be any good for you?" That's the point I've been trying to make for the last 87 pages of this book—exercise doesn't have to be painful, exhausting or injury-prone to be beneficial. Walking is the safest, most beneficial exercise in the world and I challenge any person alive to refute that fact. Walking produces *much gain without pain*—now that's *sane!*

III. WALK, DON'T DIET

"There are only two ways to lose weight effectively. One is to eat less and the other is to walk more. If you want to stay fit, trim and healthy, then follow a low cholesterol, high fiber diet, combined with a walking program.

Fred A. Stutman, M.D.
DIETWALK®, Philadelphia: Medical
Manor Books®, 1983

"OH NO! NOT ANOTHER DIET AGAIN!"

CHAPTER 7

IT'S NO FUN BEING FAT

BABY, THAT'S NOT BABY FAT!

After 3 years of age, baby fat is not baby fat any-more. If children stay fat after age 3, they run a 50 percent chance of being fat adults. Today's lifestyles have led to a new generation of fat children. Kids watch TV all day, their mothers drive them every-where, they play less sports and active games and they develop sedentary habits before they're adults.

Childhood obesity according to most health authorities can lead to:

1. Hypertension even in school children
2. Heart and kidney disease
3. Abnormal bone structure during bone growth
4. Diabetes in children with a genetic predisposition
5. Emotional problems including an increased suicide rate in fat teenagers
6. More frequent tonsil infections because of fat deposits around the tonsil tissue
7. Fat children who become fat adults, in general, don't live as long as thin kids who stay thin.

Encourage your children to go out and play. Discourage sitting in front of the TV all day. If necessary, purchase a TV lock and then you can monitor what shows they watch and the total amount of hours they spend in front of the boob-tube. Send them to the store frequently so they begin to know what their feet were made for. *Walk, don't drive them,* and you'll really be a friend.

CHILDHOOD CHOLESTEROL CAUTION

In a recent study reported in The New England Journal of Medicine, it was conclusively found that heart disease can actually begin in childhood. The study was based on the autopsies of 35 youngsters ages 11-23, who died of causes other than heart disease.

The findings indicated that the higher the level of cholesterol in the blood, the more fatty deposits that were found in the arteries. In six cases the blood cholesterol level and the amount of fat found in the arteries was comparable to that found in adults with heart disease. Three of those studied also had been known to have high blood pressure, and their arteries showed even more cholesterol deposits than those who had had normal blood pressure.

In this study, the type of cholesterol that blocked up the arteries was the LDL form of cholesterol, otherwise known as the bad-cholesterol. As we'll see later in this chapter, this type of cholesterol can be lowered by eating a low cholesterol and low saturated fat diet. Recent medical research has shown that *walking* will also lower this form of bad cholesterol (LDL), as well as raise the good cholesterol (HDL). This HDL-cholesterol can help to carry away the fatty deposits that have already started to form in the arteries.

The only way to prevent heart disease from occurring in adults is to prevent it from starting in childhood. Children should be encouraged to stay away from fatty foods, particularly fatty meats, whole milk and dairy products. The only way you can accomplish this is to set the example early in life for the whole family's eating habits. Encourage fresh fruits and vegetables, fish and fowl, whole grained cereals and breads, fat free milk and dairy products, and whole grained baked goods and pastas. Check the 10 fabulous foods for fantastic health that start with an **F**, at the end of this chapter.

Never hesitate to ask your doctor to check your child's blood cholesterol, especially if there is a family history of heart disease. The prevention of high blood cholesterol must begin in childhood if we are to make any progress in the fight against heart disease. And finally make sure your children walk or play actively every day. Let's not give the LDL (bad) cholesterol a chance to block up your child's arteries. A walk every day will help to keep cholesterol away.

BEING FAT CAN BE FATAL

The American Heart Association report stated that more than 45 million Americans have one or more forms of cardiovascular disease.

One out of every four or five adults, or approximately 40 million Americans, have **high blood pressure** and less than half of them know they have it. In 1985 over 25 thousand people died from high blood pressure's complications (stroke, heart failure, heart attacks and kidney disease).

Heart attacks were responsible for over one-half million deaths in 1985. Approximately 1 million Americans will have a heart attack this year and more than one-fourth of them will die.

Strokes were reported as the second leading cause of deaths from cardiovascular disease, which claimed over 150,000 lives in 1985. More than half of these could have been prevented by the proper treatment of hypertension.

High blood pressure, heart disease and strokes account for more than 50% of all deaths that occur in the United States every year. In most cases these diseases are caused by the accumulation of fat deposits in the arteries *(atherosclerosis)*. Fat people usually have high levels of blood fats and this is directly related to the development of atherosclerosis. This build-up of fat eventually leads to heart attacks, strokes and hypertension. The following chart—**ATHEROSCLERO-SIS**—shows what happens inside your body as your arteries get blocked with fat (Fig. 2). It's no fun to be fat, and it's even less humorous to be dead.

KEEP YOUR BODY LEAN AND YOUR ARTERIES CLEAN

Foods that are of **plant origin** do not contain cholesterol. These include fruits, vegetables, grains, cereals, nuts, and vegetable oils (coconut oil and palm oil are two exceptions which incidentally are used in baked goods, snack foods and deep-fried foods). Always choose liquid or unsaturated vegetable oils, rather than solid or hydrogenated vegetable oil products, since these **polyunsaturated** liquid oils help to lower your blood cholesterol. Safflower oil, sunflower oil and corn oil are excellent choices. These polyunsaturated oils have no cholesterol in them. They also help to lower excessive amounts of cholesterol that the body itself manufactures.

Saturated fats, on the other hand, include products of **animal origin**. These fats are found in eggs, milk, butter, cheese, dairy products, meat, fowl and fish. These saturated fats are also found in some vegetable products which include table spreads (margarine) and shortenings which have been *hydrogenated* (changing liquid oils into solids or semi-solids). Al-

FIGURE 2

ATHEROSCLEROSIS

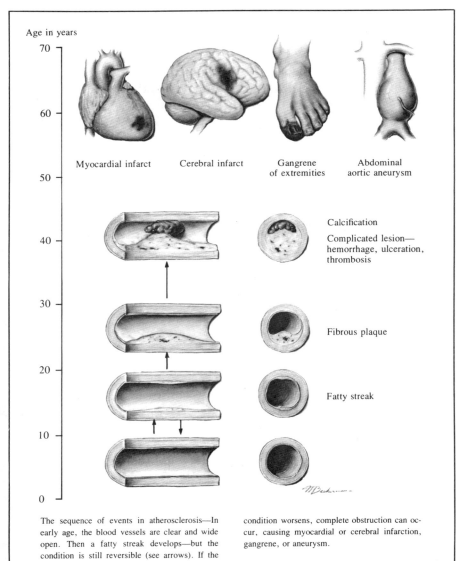

Age in years

Myocardial infarct   Cerebral infarct   Gangrene of extremities   Abdominal aortic aneurysm

Calcification
Complicated lesion—hemorrhage, ulceration, thrombosis

Fibrous plaque

Fatty streak

The sequence of events in atherosclerosis—In early age, the blood vessels are clear and wide open. Then a fatty streak develops—but the condition is still reversible (see arrows). If the condition worsens, complete obstruction can occur, causing myocardial or cerebral infarction, gangrene, or aneurysm.

©Romaine Pierson Pubs., Inc.

"Courtesy of Medical Times"

though this hydrogenation process makes these products useful for table spreads and shortenings, it however changes them from polyunsaturated fats to saturated fats. Since these saturated fats raise both the total fat content and the cholesterol levels in our bodies, they should be avoided in our diets.

Limiting the amount of **cholesterol** and **saturated fat** in our diets has two major benefits. First of all it helps you keep a lean, trim figure. Secondly, it helps to prevent strokes, heart attacks and hypertension, since these illnesses are associated with high blood levels of cholesterol. The American diet is higher in fat content than any other country in the world. This increased fat intake in our diet is responsible for the development of obesity, as well as many other fat-related disorders. A gram of dietary fat supplies your body with 9 calories compared to only 4 calories per gram of protein or carbohydrate. Since fat is such a concentrated source of calories, it is obvious that by cutting down your total fat intake, you will also cut down on the total amount of calories that you consume. Result: *body lean—arteries clean!*

SHE GOT HER JUST DESSERTS

What's as American as a piece of mother's apple pie: The answer is **cheesecake**. According to a new survey by the Gallup Poll, cheesecake is now ordered more often than apple pie for dessert. Americans, take heart—or cheesecake will take it from you. The average slice of cheesecake contains approximately 625 calories, 35 grams of total fat and 21 grams of saturated fat to clog up your arteries. No wonder. It's made from heavy cream, whole eggs, cream cheese and sugar.

However, good old **American apple pie** even with the crust has approximately 200 calories and only 3-4 grams of fat in each piece. Even better still, just an apple by itself is the best dessert of all. Apples contain **pectin** which is a natural fiber that lowers blood cholesterol. Pectin fiber also helps to slow the emptying of food from the stomach by adding bulk to the stomach lining. This accounts for the reason that apple pie or a juicy red apple satisfies the hunger control mechanism (**appestat**), whereas cheesecake with its high sugar content, stimulates an increased hunger for more food.

Take an apple any day as your first choice of a dessert since it's low in calories and high in fiber. If you must cheat, then a piece of apple pie is better than most gooey desserts. Remove the crust and you're home free! Better yet, *Walk, Don't Die,* and hold the pie.

NOW SKIM IS REALLY IN!

In a new study at the Memorial Sloan-Kettering Cancer Center in New York City, calcium has been shown to help protect adults from getting cancer of the colon. It appears that calcium neutralizes bile acids which can irritate the lining of the colon and trigger the growth of abnormal cells. The calcium content of two glasses of fat-free (skim) milk daily seems to be adequate to neutralize these potentially dangerous bile acids. Skim milk is also particularly effective in preventing thinning of the bones (osteoporosis) in older people without adding the additional fat present in regular milk. Even low-fat milk has anywhere from 2-5 grams of fat in each glass. Remember skim milk is cholesterol-free.

There is also recent evidence that calcium is effective in helping to lower blood pressure in people with hypertension. Even more startling is a new study stating that drinking three glasses of skim milk a day may give some protection against Alzheimer's disease. It appears that skim milk's calcium may counteract the effects of aluminum on the brain, which is thought to cause nerve degeneration.

One of the puzzling studies in medicine has been the eating habits of the Maasai tribesmen in Africa. Although these men regularly consumed 4-5 quarts of fermented milk daily, they had surprisingly low levels of blood cholesterol and very little coronary artery disease. It was concluded that the fermented milk had some unknown property that lowered cholesterol. However, the fact still remains that these African tribesmen walk more in one day then most of us walk in a month or more.

Dr. Haruo Kiyosawa, from the <u>Sapporo Medical College, Japan</u>, tested various milk products to see if they had a cholesterol-lowering effect. Only **skim milk**, of all products studied, lowered blood cholesterol. In addition, the skim milk actually lowered the *"bad cholesterol (LDL)"* and the *serum triglycerides* ("sugar fats")—both of which can cause blocked coronary arteries. Aside from the low fat content of skim milk, the precise explanation for these other positive findings are still under study. But until all the final results are in, it pays to drink skim. And follow the example of the African Maasai tribe and *Walk, Don't Die!*

AMERICA'S STARTING TO THINK LEAN

According to the U.S. Department of Agriculture, the dietary habits of Americans have changed significantly in the past 20 years. Although we are consuming more total calories, we are shifting our eating habits to more nutritious foods. The shift away from animal products has been motivated primarily by health concerns. Keep up the good work, America, and remember to **walk off those extra calories**.

AMERICA'S DIETARY HABITS - 1963 VS. 1983

CALORIES CONSUMED (per person, per day)

1963	————————————————— 3,180
1983	————————————————————— 3,450

FOOD CONSUMED (per person, per year)

All Food

1963	————————————————— 1,368 lb.
1983	————————————————————— 1,417 lb.

Meat

1963	————————————— 154 lb.
1983	———————————— 151 lb.

Fish

1963	———————————— 11 lb.
1983	————————————— 13 lb.

Poultry

1963	———————— 38 lb.
1983	—————————————— 66 lb.

Eggs

1963	————————————————— 309 eggs
1983	————————————— 254 eggs

Vegetables

1963	————————————— 187 lb.
1983	——————————————— 207 lb.

Fruits

1963	————————————— 120 lb.
1983	————————————— 143 lb.

Flour, Cereals

1963	————————————— 144 lb.
1983	————————————— 150 lb.

Coffee

1963	————————————— 38 gal.
1983	——————— 26 gal.

Sweeteners

1963	————————————— 111 lb.
1983	—————————————— 136 lb.

Milk

1963	———————————————— 33 gal.
1983	———————————— 27 gal.

*   *   *

GET THE FAT OUT OF YOUR FACE!

A recent report by the National Heart, Lung and Blood Institute showed that over 100,000 lives could be saved every year by just lowering cholesterol to a level of 180-200 mg. It is estimated that more than 35 million Americans have high blood cholesterol. A related study by the American College of Cardiology (3/84) showed that arteries which were blocked with cholesterol could actually reopen again after people went on a low cholesterol diet.

The following are the new dietary recommendations for a healthy heart:

A. **Limit fat to 25-30 percent of daily calories.**

Most Americans consume more than 40 percent of their daily calories as fat. This amount should be reduced to 25-30 percent with only 10 percent of the fat calories coming from saturated fats (animal fats and whole milk dairy products, including cheeses, coconut and cocoa beans and solid vegetable oils).

B. **Limit cholesterol intake to 250-300 mg daily.**

Egg yolk is the most concentrated source of cholesterol in the American diet (274 mg in one egg yolk). Liver and other organ meats are very high. Shellfish, although low in saturated fat, is relatively high in cholesterol and should be limited to once every other week.

C. **Limiting protein to 20-25 percent of all calories daily.**

Poultry without skin and fish are excellent sources of protein and are low in saturated fats.

Plant protein such as beans, soybeans and legumes are also good sources of protein.

D. **Increasing complex carbohydrates to 45-50 percent of calories consumed daily.**

Whole grain bread, cereal and pasta products, vegetables, legumes and fruits all provide excellent sources of vitamins, minerals and complex carbohydrates without fat.

E. **A low cholesterol, low saturated fat diet** will lower the **bad-cholesterol (LDL)** in the bloodstream, and prevent it from clogging up your arteries. **Walking** also helps to lower this bad-cholesterol (LDL) in your bloodstream.

F. A regular walking program will also raise the **good-cholesterol (HDL)** in your blood, which helps to remove the build-up of fat deposits in your blood vessels.

G. Follow the 10 Fabulous Foods that First start with an "**F**" For Fantastic Health:

1. Fruit
2. Fresh vegetables
3. Fish
4. Fowl
5. Fettuccini (pastas, especially whole grain)
6. Fiber (whole grain breads and cereals, legumes and beans, seeds and nuts, and bran foods)
7. Flour (whole grain oat, wheat, corn, barley and bran)
8. Fat-free milk, cheeses, yogurt and mayonnaise
9. Fabulous fakes (Egg Beaters®—Fleishman Division, Nabisco Brands, Inc.; Butter Buds®—Cumberland Packing Corp.; imitation mayonnaise, imitation cream cheese, etc.)
10. Fluids (water, fruit juices, skim milk, decaffeinated teas, coffee and soda)

THOSE WHO ONLY SAT, FOUND IT FATAL TO GET FAT

In the majority of cases obesity results from too little exercise and too much food. Life insurance studies have shown that excess weight causes cardiovascular disease with increased mortality. These same studies also reveal that life expectancy improves following weight reduction.

Obese people have a significantly higher incidence of hypertension than non-obese persons. The excess body weight demands a higher cardiac output (pumping out blood) to meet the increased metabolism of the fat person's body. This in turn causes the left ventricle chamber of the heart to gradually enlarge because of this extra workload. The combined effect of obesity, hypertension and heart enlargement may eventually lead to heart failure and death. Weight reduction can lower both the systolic and diastolic blood pressures if it is acccomplished before the complications of heart enlargement and heart failure occur.

Obesity also causes an alteration of the body chemistry and metabolism. The blood sugar goes up dramatically with obesity often leading to the development of diabetes. The uric acid in the blood becomes elevated, often leading to kidney stones and attacks of gout. Fat people have higher levels of triglycerides (sugar fats) and the bad LDL-cholesterol. They also have lower blood levels of the good HDL-cholesterol. These altered blood fats will eventually lead to severe coronary artery disease. These abnormal blood chemistries can be reversed to normal levels, if weight reduction occurs before permanent complications result.

And if all these risks of being fat weren't bad enough, here's another piece of fat to chew on. Obesity just by itself has been listed as an independent risk factor for coronary heart disease. Newer data from the 26-year follow-up statistics in the Framingham Heart Study (Hubert, 1983) demonstrated that obesity just by itself was enough to cause a significant increase in the risk of coronary heart disease and premature death in both men and women.

Had enough fat to chew on? You certainly know by now all of the risks of being fat, unless of course you don't care about living too long. And by now you should also know that there are only two ways to lose weight effectively. One is to shut your mouth and the other is to move your feet. And since most of us can only shut our mouths long enough to reach the next meal, then we had better get out there and walk every day like our lives depended on it. Walking is the only permanent weight reducer known to man or woman that can be continued for a lifetime.

> The results are now finally in
> It certainly pays to be thin
> So if you want your lifetime to last
> Then you'd better start walking fast
> Remember that those who only sat
> Found it was fatal to get fat
> Because when they got obese
> They all developed heart disease
> But those who always walked
> They lived long enough to talk
> Remember, life is wonderful and sweet
> If you want to prolong it, move your feet

**"THE FALL PROBABLY KILLED HIM BUT HE DID
HAVE A <u>VERY</u> HIGH CHOLESTEROL LEVEL"**

CHAPTER 8

DEATH DEFYING DIETS

"I'LL START MY DIET ON MONDAY MORNING"

I'll bet you've told yourself a hundred times or more, "I'll start my diet on Monday morning." How many new fad diets or quick-weight loss schemes have you begun and then discarded? And, how many times have you lost those unwanted pounds, only to have them miraculously reappear with a few extra pounds to boot?

New diet books and gimmick diet plans appear almost daily to confuse matters even worse. These plans all promise rapid weight loss, with a minimum of effort on your part. You'd almost expect the weight to come tumbling off as you read about their secret recipes, diet tips, magic potions and gimmick weight-loss plans. The truth of the matter is that the fast, easy, painless, rapid weight loss program does not exist. Rapid weight loss always ends in rapid weight gain.

And what's more, these fad diets are dangerous to your health. Most of these pseudo-scientific diet schemes give just enough nutritional information to make them sound plausible. However, if you examine them closely, you'll find they are all nutritionally unsound. We'll review a number of these death-defying fad diets and gimmick diet aids and show you why they are worthless for permanent weight loss and how they can be hazardous to your health.

I. DANGEROUS DIET-AIDS DIG GRAVES

The following group of so-called diet-aids which are designed to help you lose weight are 100% worthless. These dangerous gimmick diet tricks will help you to destroy your body as you lose weight. Many people have slimmed down into early graves using these dangerous diet aids.

1. DANGEROUS DIET DREAM DRINKS

The fasting craze or very-low-calorie diets (**VLC**) are extremely dangerous and are actually *death-defying dieting stunts*. Combined with the variety of *powdered and liquid, vitamin-mineral & protein mixes* these diets promise fast weight loss. What they don't tell their unsuspecting customers is that the weight loss is temporary and that the diet is hazardous to their health. The Food and Drug Administration is still investigating thousands of complaints of illness from consumers and hundreds of deaths from heart failure, attributable to these gimmick diets.

The side effects of these VLC diets and protein mix diets range from dry skin and vitamin deficiencies to low blood pressure and heart rate irregularities apparently caused by loss of potassium from the body. These diets also may cause protein and electrolyte depletion in the body leading to muscle, kidney, liver and heart abnormalities. Reports of hair-loss, gum disorders, loose teeth, skin rashes, brittle nails, intestinal problems and bleeding abnormalities are just a few of the side effects from these protein mixes.

Let's leave this type of diet to the professional stunt-men and women who get paid to take chances with their lives. The rest of us can lose weight safely without the need to resort to these death-defying diet stunts. The only people who come out ahead with these get-rich, get-thin programs are the diet-hustlers who are selling these diet-dream mixes to the unsuspecting public. Tell them to take their protein powders and mix them.

2. FASTING:
HOW TO WASTE YOUR WAIST!

Is dieting wearing you down? Yes, literally, according to a recent study from the University of Toronto. After 10 days of crash dieting (under 500 calories a day) actual **muscle damage** occurred, even though the dieter took a multivitamin-mineral supplement. The first symptom of muscle damage was marked *fatigue*.

The metabolic balance of *enzymes and calcium* in the muscles were abnormally changed during this period of fasting. After the muscles became clogged with calcium they were unable to relax after they had contracted. Microscopic signs of *atrophy* (death of small muscle cells) actually occurred during this process.

Acute signs of *malnutrition* were seen after only 2 weeks of fasting even in the most obese dieter. *Blood pressure* was also markedly decreased (postural hypotension) during this period. These conditions were brought about by the lack of adequate protein, carbohydrate and fat in the diet. And to make matters even worse, the dieters gained back all of their weight plus some additional pounds to spare in 6 weeks after they stopped dieting. **What a waste to waste your waist!**

3. AMPHETAMINES

Amphetamines which are prescription drugs only, have been reported to be associated with the following: hypertension, seizures, anxiety, confusion, paranoia, mania and even homicidal behavior. There are many different types of amphetamines; however, they are all prescription drugs and are potentially dangerous. They are also sold on the street under a variety of names—speed, uppers, black beauties, etc.

Amphetamines have also been reported to cause many heart disorders ranging from palpitations to heart attacks and heart failure. These side effects can occur even with small doses. Combined with other drugs and alcohol, they repeatedly have caused deaths from respiratory and heart failure. If your doctor prescribes amphetamines for appetite suppression, I'd suppress him by finding another doctor.

4. GRAPEFRUIT BURNERS & STARCH BLOCKERS

The newest entries into the gimmick diet field are the so called "starch blockers and grapefruit burners." The promotors of these tablets claim they block starch digestion and burn calories thus promoting weight loss. There is no medical evidence that these starch blockers and grapefruit burners have any value in weight reduction. The FDA has recently ruled that these tablets should be considered drugs and not food products and therefore need to be tested before they can be marketed.

There have been several medical studies that have found no evidence of blocked starch digestion or reduced calorie absorption from either of these products. In other words, these tablets are virtually worthless as weight-loss aids, and both types are potentially hazardous to your health.

The FDA has also received many reports of side effects from both of these products, including nausea, vomiting, diarrhea, abdominal cramps, headaches, dizziness and blurring of vision. More serious reactions also have been reported including both liver and pancreas damage, death from an acute inflammation of the pancreas, intestinal obstruction and bleeding stomach ulcers.

Yet on the back page of most magazines and newspapers in the country, you'll be able to find a full page ad about one of these products. "Burn fat while you sleep." "Eat all you want and lose weight." As long as the diet promoters pay for the ads, these newspapers and magazines don't care what they print. Good old Yankee ingenuity—"If it's in print, it must be true."

5. DRUGSTORE DIET PILLS

In every drugstore across America, you can find shelf after shelf filled with hundreds of different colored over-the-counter (no prescription needed) diet pills. Americans spend millions of dollars each year for these worthless, potentially hazardous diet aids. The Center for Science in the Public Interest wants the Food and Drug Administration to make the common ingredient found in these diet pills—phenylpropanolamine (PPA) a prescription drug. The companies that make these pills have primarily one interest—to make money. They don't care a hill-of-pills about your health.

A recent medical report in Medical World News stated that high doses of *phenylpropanolamine* (PPA), found in these over-the-counter diet pills, may be associated with strokes and other serious disorders. These pills, which have amphetamine-like effects, have been known to produce symptoms of paranoia, confusion, headaches and emotional disorders. High blood pressure, heart irregularities, kidney failure, convulsions, strokes, and even homicidal behavior have also been reported as side effects from the use of these pills. If you take these diet pills you may lose more than just a few pounds—you may lose your life!

6. CELLULITE: THE FANCY FAT

Many so-called diet authorities claim that **cellulite** is a different kind of fat requiring special treatment to get rid of it. The truth of the matter is that fat is fat, and cellulite is actually a mythical term made up by Hollywood celebrities. When you eat too much, fat cells immediately beneath the skin enlarge, and the strands of fibrous tissue that connect these fat cells may not stretch. Ordinary fat then gets a lumpy appearance on the hips, thighs and lower abdomen. This unfortunately is a genetic trait—some women develop these lumpy deposits and others don't.

If you take fat biopsies (small pieces of tissue) from people with these lumpy fatty deposits and also from people with regular fat deposits, all of the biopsy specimens will be identified under the microscope as **ordinary fat cells**. Fat is fat! There is no such thing as cellulite.

The gimmick remedies designed to treat this non-existent condition include vibrating machines, body wrappings, massages, suction machines and a whole range of phony diet and exercise tricks. Many are completely harmless and others are highly dangerous, often leading to broken blood vessels and bleeding under the skin. Occasionally these hemorrhages can lead to blood clots which could travel through the blood vessels to the heart or lungs causing death.

The Food & Drug Administration has published a

booklet entitled "Cellulite," in order to protect the public from charlatans claiming treatments for a non-existent disorder. You can write to the Consumer Information Center, Dept. 560K, Pueblo, CO 81009 for a free copy of this booklet.

II. DEATH-DEFYING FAD DIETS

Most weight-loss programs which have no scientific or nutritional basic principles can be classified as "fad diets." They promise quick weight loss with little regard for the health of the dieter. A diet that recommends an increased intake of one particular type of food (example—pasta), while limiting other food groups is nutritionally a bad, fad diet. These diets are nutritionally unsound and they are potentially dangerous. After some weight is initally lost, a plateau is reached wherein no further weight is lost. Discouraged with the results, the dieter starts to eat again because of depression and anxiety and gains more weight than he/she originally lost (rebound phenomenon). Let's take a look at some of the common death-defying fad diets and the bad side effects that they can cause, including death.

1. LOW CARBOHYDRATE DIETS

Low-carbohydrate diets are one of the most common forms of death-defying diets. They have a variety of different names: water diets, drinking man's diets, quick weight-loss diets, bacon and eggs diets, high fat diets, etc. They all are basically **low in carbohydrates** and **high in fat and protein**. Another serious problem with these diets is that they're low in fiber and that can result in serious stomach and intestinal problems. Low fiber diets can also cause heart and

blood vessel diseases by raising cholesterol to dangerous levels in the blood.

These diets may lead to a metabolic condition
known as *ketosis* which is actually the same disorder
that occurs in diabetics. This condition may have the
following **side effects**: general weakness, lack of stam-
ina and strength, nausea and vomiting, dehydration,
loss of calcium from the body, mental clouding and
memory loss, muscle cramps and fainting.

More serious disorders that have been reported are:
kidney disorders and kidney failure in those people
with underlying kidney disease; heart beat irregularities, heart attacks and strokes caused by the build-up
of cholesterol in the arteries; and high blood pressure
and vascular disease.

These diets may result in early rapid weight loss,
which in turn produces *rapid weight gain* when the
diet is stopped. For each gram of sugar stored in the
body, *3 grams of water* are also stored. These low carbohydrate diets cause the body to rapidly lose sugar thus
causing a rapid water weight loss, not body fat. When
the sugar reservoir runs out, the water loss stops and
then the weight loss stops. The dieters then rapidly
regain their weight with some additional pounds to
spare, after they become discouraged and resume normal eating habits (rebound phenomenon).

2. LOW PROTEIN DIETS

The low protein or high carbohydrate diets are
another common type of quick weight-loss diets. They
all have the same unsound nutritional basis: **low in
protein** and **high in carbohydrates and fat**. They
are called by a variety of different names: grapefruit
diets, fruit and enzyme diets, salad diets, vegetarian
diets, cabbage diets, fasting diets, big city suburban
diets, pasta diets, etc.

The body literally consumes itself from within on

a diet deficient in protein. Early in the course of the diet, the **hair** becomes fine and thin and loses its natural luster. Then the **nails** become brittle and cracked and slow their growth rate. Eventual loss of protein from the **skin, muscles** and **internal organs** results in easy bruising, muscle weakness and malfunction of the internal organs. These diets are usually deficient in many essential **vitamins and minerals** which may cause diarrhea and aggravate pre-existing stomach and intestinal problems.

The human body has *no mechanism for storing protein.* Weight loss which results from this type of diet, causes a loss of *muscle tissue* as well as fat which is a dangerous situation. When weight is rapidly regained after stopping the diet, the lost muscle tissue is usually replaced with *fat.* These diets usually caution the dieter not to stay on the diet too long because of dangerous side effects. The dieters, in turn, should caution the authors of these dangerous diets to get out of town and stick to hairdressing, acting, or whatever else they were trained to do.

3. HIGH PROTEIN DIETS

These diets allow you to eat unlimited amounts of meat, eggs, cheese and all foods high in animal protein. This diet is high in cholesterol and saturated fats and can lead to heart attacks and strokes.

These diets are lacking in essential vitamins and minerals because fruits, vegetables and grain cereals are excluded. This type of diet is also low in fiber causing intestinal and stomach problems and the build-up of cholesterol in your arteries.

The high protein diet is particularly dangerous because it puts extra stress on the kidneys and urinary tract. The high concentration of protein in the blood may result in spillover in the urine and this protein strains the kidneys' filtering system.

4. WATER DIETS

Many diet plans advocate drinking from six to twelve 8 oz. glasses of water daily combined with the diet plan. In the majority of people this will have no adverse effect on their health. However, according to a recent medical study, patients who were prone to develop **seizures** (for example, epileptics) may experience an increase in seizure activity (convulsions) when they drink large quantities of water (eight to twelve 8 oz. glasses per day). These people should restrict the amount of water they drink daily according to their own physician's recommendation and should not begin any diet or exercise program without consulting their doctor.

Even if you have no history of any medical disorder you should always check with your own personal physician before starting any diet program. Any diet that advocates excessive amounts of any food or substance even including excess water intake could be potentially dangerous if you have a particular medical problem. For example, some types of heart and kidney problems where fluid retention is common, may be adversely affected by drinking excessive quantities of water.

5. ENZYME CATALYST DIET

The grapefruit, pineapple, strawberry, pumpkin, carrot, banana, and other fruit and vegetable diets are all variations of the same gimmick hillbilly diet. They claim to melt fat cells and wash them right out of the body. These diets are based on unsubstantiated unscientific "enzyme laws." The authors of these diets haven't the foggiest idea of what an enzyme actually is. They also claim that certain undigested food gets stuck in the body and promotes the development of fat—pure hog-wash!

These diets are not only nutritionally unsound, they are downright dangerous. They can cause severe diarrhea, dehydration, electrolyte abnormalities and even heart irregularities. This type of diet also promotes binge eating where the rebound weight gain is faster than the initial weight loss, which incidentally is only water loss anyway. I'd rename these fruit and vegetable diets—*garbage diets!*

6. BULIMIA

A surprisingly large number of women have used this so-called "binge and purge" syndrome to control or lose weight. These people have definite psychological problems and exhibit symptoms of chronic anxiety and depression. They usually go on binge eating splurges, eating anywhere from 1,500-4,000 calories at a time. The foods eaten usually are high calorie foods (candy, cake, ice cream, any fatty food, pizza, soda, etc.). They usually skip a meal prior to their binge eating episodes.

Following their binge eating, the bulimic persons induce vomiting to rid themselves of the huge quantities of food they have eaten. These people develop many serious side effects from this abnormal behavior dieting technique. Many women develop severe hormonal imbalances and menstrual irregularities. Other chemical imbalances include loss of potassium from the body and a serious disorder known as metabolic alkalosis caused by the loss of chloride from the stomach. There have also been many cases of severe dental problems (caused by stomach acid eroding the teeth) and marked swelling of the salivary glands in the mouth and face.

Several cases of heart rhythm abnormalities and sudden cardiac deaths have also been reported. Many of these cardiac deaths are due to a type of heart condition known as *cardiomyopathy*. This disorder results from the repeated use of the drug—*ipecac*, which is often taken by the bulimic person to induce vomiting. These people require medical and psychiatric treatment.

7. LAXATIVE ABUSE FOR WEIGHT REDUCTION

Another common method of attempting to control weight is by the repeated use of laxatives. These people, like bulimic persons also have deep-seated psychological problems. They also go on binge eating spurts and then try to rid the body of these foods by using strong laxatives and cathartics.

This dangerous attempt at weight reduction is completely ineffective and has serious side effects associated with it. Laxative abuse can cause permanent damage to the nerve fibers in the intestine, often resulting in intestinal bleeding. It can also result in the impairment of the absorption of calcium, magnesium, iron, potassium and zinc from the intestine. This eventually leads to severe chemical imbalances in the body. These people also require medical and often psychiatric counseling.

8. ANOREXIA NERVOSA

This complicated deep-seated psychological and medical problem is a combination of behavioral disturbances (weight phobia, addiction to starvation and occasionally self-induced vomiting and laxative abuse). These individuals usually begin to become overly concerned about their weight during their teens. They all suffer from a psychological weight phobia—"fear of getting fat." These people usually have severe emotional problems and have difficulty relating to family and friends. They begin by saying that they are just dieting, even though their weights may be normal. This so-called diet often progresses to actual starvation techniques with resultant malnutrition. The anorectics will deny the fact that they are starving themselves, usually saying that they are getting more than enough to eat.

The side effects result from severe malnutrition. These patients become emaciated and often develop convulsions, hair loss, muscle atrophy, loss of menstruation, insomnia, electrolyte and chemical imbalances, heart irregularities, adrenal and thyroid gland abnormalities, psychoses and many other serious disorders including death from malnutrition. This condition often affects teenagers and requires long-term intensive medical, nutritional and psychiatric supportive therapy.

* * *

All these death-defying fad diets and gimmick diet aids bring in over 100 million dollars yearly to diet promotors. The so-called diet authorities who invent these schemes are not in the least concerned with your health or your death for that matter. Their primary concern is to make a fast buck and then quickly get out of town when the reports of the side effects start coming in. Once they have your money they could care less what you say about them. The majority of charlatans who promote these diets haven't the foggiest idea of what good, safe nutrition is all about and most of them only have degrees in making money. Even many of the doctor diet books are written by physicians whose licenses should have expired before they did. The last time many of them read a scientific book was back in medical school.

Special protein drinks, diet drugs, weight-loss clinics, and quick weight-loss fad diets are all diet gimmicks. They promise you permanent weight-loss;

however the only thing that loses fat permanently is your wallet. Each diet plan also promises quick weight loss. What they fail to tell you is that you will gain weight just as quickly when you stop their plan, providing that you don't get sick or die first. Fad diets and gimmick diet aids have one thing in common—they are extremely dangerous and can cause disease, disability and even death. Why risk life or limb to lose a few pounds? *Walking* will keep you thin if you try it, just **Walk, Don't Diet!**

"COUNTING CALORIES MAKES ME HUNGRY."

CHAPTER 9

DIETSTEP®: W.O.W.—WHAT A DIET!

THE FAT FORMULA

The latest report from the National Institutes of Health meeting in Bethesda, MD (Feb., 1985) again confirmed that obesity is a *major health risk*. The evidence is strong that obesity not only shortens life, but it actually affects the quality of life also.

Almost 20 percent of Americans are overweight. How can you tell if you're one of them? It's simple—just follow the **fat formula**:

Females—100 lbs. for the first 5 feet in height, plus 5 lbs. for each additional inch. Example: 5′2″ = 110 lbs.

Males—106 lbs. for the first 5 feet in height, plus 6 lbs. for each additional inch. Example 5′9″ = 160 lbs.

The increased medical risks for being overweight are: *hypertension, heart attack, stroke, diabetes, arthritis, cancer of all types, and increased surgical risks* if you need an operation. These risks seem to be even worse if most of your weight is carried in the upper body (chest, hips and abdomen) rather than in the buttocks and legs.

If you flunk the fat formula, just **Walk-Off-Weight** using the **Dietstep® Plan. W.O.W.**—what a diet! Let's put felonius fat where it belongs—off the street and behind bars.

"I DON'T EAT THAT MUCH!"

The question I get asked most often from patients about being overweight is—"How come I keep gaining weight? I don't eat that much." Well, the truth of the matter is that we get fatter as we get older because our physical activity tends to decrease even though our food intake stays the same. The only way to beat the battle of the bulge is to burn those unwanted pounds away. Walking actually **burns calories**. The following table will give you an idea as to the energy expended in walking, which is actually the number of calories burned per minute or per hour (**TABLE I**).

TABLE I

WALKING SPEEDS	CALORIES BURNED/ MINUTE	CALORIES BURNED/ 30 MINUTES	CALORIES BURNED/ HOUR
Slow speed (2 mph)	4-5	120-150	240-300
Brisk speed (3 mph)	5-6	150-180	300-360
Fast speed (4 mph)	6-7	180-210	360-420
Race walking (5 mph)	7-8	210-250	420-500

After a large meal, especially around the holidays, many people will say—"It doesn't matter how much I eat, I'll work it off after dinner by shoveling the walk, or jogging, or playing football with the kids." Heavy exercise immediately after a meal is one of the leading causes of heart attacks in middle-aged and older people. The accident wards in all of the hospitals throughout the country are stacked up with coronaries, immediately after the big Thanksgiving and Christmas dinners. Strenuous exercise after a large meal causes the increased supply of blood in the stomach and intestinal tract to be diverted to the exercising muscles. This puts a strain on the cardiovascular system especially in anyone who has a heart or circulatory problem. This is often the first time that many of these people become aware that they have a heart condition, and unfortunately in many cases the last.

A calm *walk*, on the other hand, 45-60 minutes after eating, does not stress the cardiovascular system and burns many of the excess calories that you should not have eaten in the first place. It's far better to get up and walk away from that big meal before you overstuff your face. When you physically walk away from the table you are removing yourself from temptation, but even more importantly, you are allowing the fullness control center in your brain to catch up to what's really going on in your stomach. You are actually full, but you don't know it yet. Remember, *eating less* and *walking more* are the only two ways to lose weight effectively.

TRIM THE FAT OFF THAT MEAT PLEASE!

A pound of body fat contains approximately *3,500 calories*. When you eat 3,500 more calories than your body actually needs, it stores up that pound as body fat. If you reduce your intake by 3,500 calories, you will lose a pound. It doesn't make any difference how long it takes your body to store or burn these 3,500 calories. The result is always the same. You either gain or lose one pound of body fat, depending on how long it takes you to accumulate or burn up 3,500 calories.

You can actually lose weight then by just walking. When you walk at a speed of 3 mph for *one hour every day,* you will burn up *350 calories* each day. Therefore, if you walk *one hour a day for 10 days,* then you will burn up a total *3,500 calories.* Since there are 3,500 calories in each pound of fat, when you burn up 3,500 calories by walking, you will lose a pound of body fat. You will *continue* to lose one pound of body fat every time you complete 10 hours of walking at a speed of 3 mph. It works every time!

THOSE WHO SAT, DIDN'T BURN FAT

If you just count calories, your chances of losing weight are minimal. *Walking,* however, is the only certain way towards permanent weight reduction. The majority of fat people are much less active than the majority of thin people. It is their sedentary life style that accounts for their excess weight and not their overeating. If they just took a brisk walk for one hour every day they could lose 18 pounds in 6 months, or 36 pounds in one year without any change in their diets.

If you want to lose weight permanently, then the energy burned during your exercise should come from *fats* and not from carbohydrates. During the first 20 minutes of moderate exercise, 2/3 of the energy burned comes from carbohydrates while only 1/3 comes from body fats. During the next 40 minutes of exercise, 2/3 of the energy burned comes from body fats and only 1/3 from carbohydrates. It stands to reason then, that longer periods of a continuous exercise like walking is better for permanent weight reduction than short spurts of strenuous exercise (examples: jogging, calisthenics, racketball, etc.).

If you increase the duration of your exercise from 20 minutes to 30-60 minutes you will burn more energy from body fats than you will burn from carbohydrates, resulting in weight-loss that really stays lost. Once you've lost your weight, you will maintain your weight-loss better by **walking** 40-60 minutes every day than by doing calisthenics or jogging for 20-30 minutes. This occurs because you will be burning a ¹ ₊ner proportion of body fats rather than carbohydrates. Remember, *those who sat, didn't burn fat.*

HUNGRY AGAIN?

Do you think exercise will make you hungry? Wrong! Exercise has an *appetite-depressing effect.* There are three reasons why exercise decreases your appetite:

1. The *flow of blood* during and immediately after exercise is shunted away from the digestive tract toward the muscles used for exercise. This decreases hunger pangs from your stomach.

2. Exercise regulates the *brain center* (Appestat) which controls the appetite. Increased exercise will decrease your appetite. Decreased exercise on the other hand will increase your appetite.

3. Your *blood sugar* is burned as a source of energy instead of blood fats during the first 20 minutes of exercise. Since blood sugar is the primary source of energy for your brain, a *low blood sugar* level will make you feel hungry. However, when you exercise for more than 20 minutes, fat begins to be released into the bloodstream and it is burned as a fuel instead of sugar to produce energy. This enables your brain's blood sugar level to remain at a normal level and consequently you will not feel hungry.

These findings show that walking decreases your appetite rather than increasing it. So if you take a 30-

60 minute walk before you sit down to eat, you'll eat less than the person who sits in front of the TV before his dinner. Remember, inactivity stimulates your brain center to make you hungry. Exercise, on the other hand, has an appetite-suppressing effect on your brain.

W.O.W.—WHAT A DIET!

Many studies have clearly documented the *weight-loss effects* of exercise. Even more important is that the weight loss caused by walking is almost all due to the *burning of body fat,* not protein. The only exceptions are a small amount of initial water loss and the burning of carbohydrates during the first 20 minutes of exercise. This weight loss or weight maintenance can be continued indefinitely as long as you walk regularly. You are literally **walking off weight (W.O.W.).**

Not only does walking *before meals* decrease your appetite, but recent studies have shown that walking approximately 45-60 minutes *after eating* increases the metabolic body rate to burn away calories at a faster rate. It appears then that walking after eating is an effective way to lose additional pounds.

This burning of calories at a faster rate has been explained as a combination of the energy expended from walking and the calories burned from the actual ingestion of food itself. This is called the **Thermic Effect of Food** or the **Specific Dynamic Action**. We actually burn more calories as we eat because the energy metabolism of the body actually increases 5-10 percent. This doesn't mean that the more you eat the more calories you'll burn. But it is a good reason for *walking 45-60 minutes after meals* for additional weight loss.

Remember, never strenuously exercise after eating, and for that matter, never exercise strenuously at
all. And remember, you were told never to even walk
after a meal. Well, we are now modifying that rule to
read—never walk immediately after eating; however if
you want to lose weight at a faster rate, then walk
before meals to cut down your appetite and walk approximately 45-60 minutes after meals to burn more
calories. Sounds good to me! **W.O.W. what a diet!**

DON'T WAIT TO LOSE WEIGHT!

THE DIETSTEP® PROGRAM is based on walking at a brisk pace (3 mph)—provided that there is *no
change* in your daily food intake. This weight-loss program is based upon *calories burned by walking only.*
By following **The DIETSTEP® PROGRAM**, you will
lose weight by actually **W**alking **O**ff **W**eight!
W.O.W.—what a diet!

Three miles per hour is a speed that can be maintained for a long duration without causing stress,
strain or fatigue. We are not talking about window-
shopping walking which is much too slow (1 mile/hr.)
and which is not at all useful in burning calories. Nor
are we suggesting fast walking (4 miles/hr.) which is
too fast to be continued for long periods of time without
tiring. And we certainly are not recommending race
walking (5 miles/hr.) which is worthless as a permanent weight reduction plan, and has all of the same
hazards and dangers that jogging has (**Table I**).

The following walking plans have been designed
for either weight loss or weight maintenance. You can
walk anywhere, any time, any place, as long as you
make the time. Remember, you can always take the
time to fit a walk into your schedule. And if you don't
have the time—make it! Don't *wait* to lose *weight*,
when just walking will make your figure look *great*.

DIETSTEP® WALKING-OFF-WEIGHT PLANS

1. DIETSTEP® PLAN #1 (LOSE A POUND EVERY 20 DAYS)

On this Dietstep® plan you will walk for **one-hour every other day** or **½-hour every day**. Walking at a brisk pace of 3 mph, you will burn up approximately **350 calories every hour** that you walk. Let's see how much weight you'll lose by this plan.

1. Walk ½ hour daily x 350 calories/hour = 175 calories burned per day.
2. Walk 3½ hours per week x 350 calories/hour = 1,225 calories burned per week.
3. Walk 10 hours every 20 days x 350 cal./hr. = 3,500 calories burned or **one pound lost every 20 days** (or 175 cal. burned per day x 20 days = 3,500 calories).

On this walking-off-weight Dietstep® plan you will lose one pound every 20 days or 18 pounds in one year. You can actually **walk off 18 pounds in one year without dieting!**

2. DIETSTEP® PLAN #2 (LOSE A POUND EVERY 10 DAYS)

On this Dietstep® plan you can lose **one pound every 10 days** by just walking **one hour every day of the week**. The only difference in this plan is that you are now walking an hour every day. You will still be burning up **350 calories** every hour that you walk briskly (3 mph).

Remember, this Dietstep® plan also works without any change in your diet. Since it takes 10 hours of walking at 3 mph to burn up 3,500 calories or one pound, if you walk for an hour every day, you will lose **one pound every 10 days**. By following this plan you can actually lose **3 pounds every month** or **36 pounds in one year**. Not bad, for just walking.

3. DIETSTEP® PLAN #3 (LOSE A POUND A WEEK)

For those of you who want to lose weight a little faster you can walk for 45 minutes twice daily. By walking a total of **1½ hours every day** of the week you will be able to speed up the walking-off-weight Dietstep® plan. When you walk 1½ hours every day, you will burn up 525 calories each day or 3,675 calories per week. You can see that you will lose a pound a week on this plan with a few extra (175 calories) to spare. You may divide your 1½ hours of walking into three 30 minute sessions daily if that's more convenient for you. The weight-loss results will be the same.

This plan will enable you to lose **one pound every 7 days**, or **4 1/3 pounds a month**, or approximately **52 pounds in a year**. Again, all this weight loss occurs without your changing one thing in your diet.

4. DIETSTEP® PLAN #4 (STAY THE SAME WEIGHT)

When you have walked off as much weight as you want to lose and are now satisfied with your present weight, then you are ready for the Dietstep® maintenance plan. You can maintain your present weight on this plan and have an **extra 175-calorie snack every day** as a bonus. Remember, you must continue walking **one-hour every other day** or ½ **hour daily** as indicated on the **Dietstep® Plan #1.** You will continue to burn up an extra 1,225 calories every week or 175 calories daily which is where your 175 calorie bonus snack comes from.

By following the Dietstep® Maintenance Plan your weight stays the same while you enjoy your 175 calorie snack every day. All you have to do is walk an hour every other day or ½ hour every day! Sound easy? It is!

5. DIETSTEP® CHEATER'S PLAN

Let's say your weight is just where you'd like it to be, but you don't want to gain another ounce. Or say your weight is nowhere near what you would like it to be, but you really can't afford to gain another pound without splitting your seams. Each of you would like to be able to cheat and at least stay the same weight. Well fear no more, the **DIETSTEP® CHEATER'S PLAN** is just for you.

How about a piece of candy, a slice of cake, french fries, a cone of ice cream, a slice of pizza or a cold beer? With **THE DIETSTEP® CHEATER'S PLAN** you have the perfect method that allows you to **cheat** without paying the price. Eat your favorite snack food, consult the following table (**TABLE II**) and walk the number of minutes listed in order to burn up the extra calories you've cheated on. The following table shows how many minutes of walking at a brisk pace (3 mph) are necessary to burn up the caloric value of those foods listed.

If your favorite snack is not listed on the following table, you can easily figure out the time you have to walk to burn off your snack's calories. Look up on any calorie counter the number of calories for your favorite snack food and divide by the number 6. This answer

TABLE II
DIETSTEP® CHEATER'S PLAN
BRISK WALKING (3 mph) BURNS SNACKS

American cheese (1 sl.)	16 minutes
apple (medium)	15 minutes
apple juice (6 oz.)	17 minutes
bagel (1)	23 minutes
banana (medium)	16 minutes
beer (12 oz.)	30 minutes
bologna sandwich	50 minutes
candy bar (1 oz.)	45 minutes
cake (1 slice pound)	63 minutes
chocolate bar/nuts (1 oz.)	28 minutes
cheese crackers (6)	35 minutes
cheese steak (med.)	55 minutes
chicken, fried (3 pieces)	50 minutes
chocolate cookies (3)	25 minutes
corn chips (small pack)	33 minutes
doughnut (jelly)	40 minutes
frankfurter & roll	50 minutes
french fries (2 oz.)	50 minutes
hamburger (4 oz.) and roll	73 minutes
ice cream cone	30 minutes
ice cream sandwich	35 minutes
ice cream sundae	75 minutes
milk shake, choc.(8 oz.)	42 minutes
muffin, blueberry	25 minutes
orange juice (6 oz.)	16 minutes
peanut butter crackers (6)	50 minutes
peanuts, in shell (2 oz.)	37 minutes
pie, apple (1 slice)	46 minutes
pizza (1 slice)	40 minutes
potato chips (small pack)	33 minutes
pretzels (hard—3 small)	30 minutes
pretzels (soft—1 Superpretzel®)	30 minutes
shrimp cocktail (6 small)	18 minutes
soda—cola (12 oz.)	24 minutes
tunafish sandwich	41 minutes
wine, chablis (4 oz.)	14 minutes
whiskey, rye (1 oz.)	17 minutes

will give you the number of minutes it takes to walk your snack off. The number 6 comes from the fact that walking at a brisk pace (3 mph) burns approximately 6 calories per minute. Example: Frankfurter and roll = 300 calories. Divide 6 into 300 and you get 50. It will take you 50 minutes to walk off this snack—"Hot Dog"!

*   *   *

By following these five Dietstep® plans you can either lose weight or maintain weight, or just cheat by walking only. Remember, it's easy to lose weight and look your best. Just do the Dietstep®!

WALK-OFF-WEIGHT AND LOOK GREAT WITH THE DIETSTEP®

STRESS—WOMEN EAT, MEN PLAY

A recent study presented at the annual meeting of the American Dietetic Association, revealed that women eat more and men engage in physical activity (sports) when confronted with stressful situations. This is probably related to the fact that women are more involved with food than men, especially if they are home more and do the food shopping. Men, on the other hand, seem to seek physical activity to dissipate aggressive feelings which result from stress. The bottom line for women: *get out and walk away from the market and the refrigerator!* Do the **DIETSTEP**®, for weight-loss and lots of pep.

YOUR MONEY OR YOUR CLOTHES!

In a recent survey conducted by <u>Glamour Magazine</u>, women would rather go on a shopping spree for new clothes than take a vacation, have a new romance or go on a diet. The findings indicate that the clothes would not only be for dress but also for work in hopes of getting a better job.

In their survey, women polled stated that their one fashion-fear would be that they would look fat in their clothes. Well, if you fall into this category, then fear not; walking will not only keep your dress size down, but it will keep you looking great in your new wardrobe without your having to go on a diet. Your trim walking figure will make you look good in anything. Remember, *walking* makes a woman look her best, when she does the **DIETSTEP®**.

"HOW ABOUT IT, MILDRED? SHOULD WE TRY
TO GET UP AND TAKE A WALK?"

IV. WALK, DON'T SIT

"Those who think they have not time enough for bodily exercise will sooner or later have to find time enough for illness."

—Hippocrates
Father of Medicine

"YES DEAR, I WALKED TODAY. I PICKED UP
A CASE OF BEER!"

CHAPTER 10

SEDENTARY SITTERS SUCCUMB SOONER

WALK, DON'T SIT

The 1985 President's Council Study on Physical Fitness in America revealed a startling discovery: the number one exercise engaged in by adults over 18 years of age was *walking*. Over 35 million people reported walking as their regular form of exercise. The other startling finding was that the only activity which had more proponents than walking, was **sitting**. More than 60% of the adult population in America reported that sitting was their number one favorite leisure activity.

Walking, without even looking like an exercise, achieves the same health and fitness benefits as other more strenuous forms of exercise—but don't tell this to the sitters. They've been brainwashed by the joggers into thinking that exercise has to be painful to be beneficial and that's why they're still sitting. Once they realize that walking is an even better exercise than jogging, then and only then will they start to get out of their chairs.

Many medical studies on longevity indicate that

we can *increase our life expectancy* as much as 10 to 15 years by following a regular program of walking; elimination of smoking, salt, saturated fats and cholesterol, alcohol and caffeine; maintenance of normal body weight; and a reduction of stress. Between the ages of 30-45, however, the majority of us become increasingly more inactive. The death rate from strokes and heart attacks is 8-10 times greater in the sedentary population than in those who walk regularly. *Walk, don't sit,* unless you're only able to rock and knit.

SEDENTARY SITTERS SUCCUMB SOONER

With the new wave of fitness clubs, aerobics classes, exercise clinics and weight machines, we are seeing new injuries, disabilities and in some cases even deaths. These new flashy so-called fitness builders are no more than glorified calisthenics, each with its own special dangers and hazards.

Inactivity, on the other hand, is just as bad if not worse for you than strenuous exercises or jogging. More and more studies have shown that there is an increased incidence of osteoporosis, arthritis, obesity, diabetes and neurological diseases in the inactive person. Sedentary people also have a significantly higher incidence of respiratory and circulatory diseases, heart disease, hypertension and strokes than people who walk regularly. Even some types of cancer (for example, colon and breast cancer) occur with greater frequency in the sedentary individual.

When the body is denied its constant fresh supply of oxygen, the individual tissues and cells begin to break down and age prematurely. Inactivity is the one sure way to an early grave. This occurs because you are not stimulating the cardiovascular and pulmonary systems to extract and distribute maximum supplies of oxygen to your cells. The individual cell's machinery is a delicate mechanism. Once the cell has been denied its full allotment of oxygen and nutrients, it begins to malfunction and show signs of permanent damage. Premature aging including early senility and depression are some of the most common findings in the sedentary person.

Walking is the only sure road to good health, physical fitness, mental alertness and a long happy life. And I guarantee you that if you take these "steps" you'll delay your death. So **Walk, Don't Die**, it's certainly worth a try. What do you have to lose—only your life!

LET'S MOVE IT!

A recent study at the State University of New York in Buffalo has now linked even **colon cancer** to a lack of physical activity. This condition had been previously thought to be caused only by a *low-fiber, high-fat diet*. Now, however, it appears that men with sedentary jobs (bus drivers, bookkeepers, accountants, computer operators, etc.) are 60 percent more likely to get cancer of the colon compared to more physically active men (longshoremen, mailmen, auto mechanics, etc.).

In this study the occupations of approximately 500 rectal and colon cancer patients were compared to the occupations of over 1,400 patients with other diseases. All of these patients were white males. Men who had spent more than 20 years in completely sedentary jobs had twice the incidence of colon cancer as compared to those men with active jobs. And men who worked at low-activity jobs had 1½ times the risk of colon cancer as active workers.

Physical activity, especially a regular *walking program*, appears to stimulate the movement of waste products through the colon, thus decreasing the time that the potential waste carcinogens are in contact with the wall of the colon. This is a similar theory to that which explains why a high-fiber, low-fat diet also helps to prevent colon cancer.

Walk, don't sit! Let's move it!

KEEP YOUR BREAST
AND ALL THE REST

A new Harvard University study found that women who exercise regularly had a significantly lower incidence of breast cancer and cancer of the reproductive organs. Over 5,000 college graduates aged 21-80 were surveyed in the study and at least half of the women had participated in college athletics. Most of the women in this study continued moderate exercises like walking after they left college. Only a very small percentage engaged in high intensity exercises like marathon running.

This study found that less active women had 2½ times as much cancer of the uterus, cervix, vagina and ovaries and almost twice as much breast cancer. The inactive women who were fatter than the active women seemed to produce more estrogen. This higher level of estrogen appears to be directly related to the higher incidence of breast and reproductive organ cancer. The leaner active women seemed to produce not only less estrogen but a less potent form of estrogen than did the fatter women.

WALKING K.O.'S COLDS AND FLU
AND MAYBE CANCER TOO!

Italian researchers now say that regular exercise like walking may actually help you fight off infections. After one hour of walking it was noted that the blood level of interferon nearly doubled in those middle-aged men who participated in the study. *Interferon* is a compound which is produced naturally in the body to help fight off virus infections.

Most of us usually go to bed and suffer in sedentary silence with a cold or flu virus. If this research is confirmed, you'll be able to put aside your chicken soup and instead go out for a brisk walk to build up your body's level of interferon. Haven't you ever noticed that the more active you are with a cold or flu, the better you feel? Only when you sit or lie down do you start to feel the aches, chills, sweats and the sniffles. Wouldn't it be amazing to cure the common cold with a brisk walk? It certainly appears from this study that interferon can help to interfere with your cold or flu.

There is also significant research being conducted on interferon's ability to inhibit certain forms of cancer. Wouldn't it be marvelous if the wonderful wizard of walking could play a role in cancer prevention too? Until all of the results are in, let's try to walk off that cold or flu and hope that walking will K.O. cancer too!

THOSE WHO SAT GOT BAD BACKS

It has been suggested that over 100 million dollars are spent each year on workmen's compensation costs, for back problems which are directly related to prolonged sitting. Back pain was the primary reason given for time lost from work on over 50% of workmen's compensation claims. And the most startling finding in this study was that office workers who sat all day had an even higher incidence of back problems than workmen who did heavy lifting and other physically demanding jobs.

Anatomically, sitting puts considerably more strain and stress on the spine than does standing or walking. When you stand, the weight of the body is supported by the back, hips and legs; therefore, the

pressure exerted on the back is evenly distributed
throughout the entire length of the spinal column.
When you walk, there is even less pressure exerted on
the spine, because the forward thrust of your body
reduces the force of gravity on your back. However,
when you sit for prolonged periods of time the weight of
your body is unevenly distributed to the low back and
hips.

Prolonged sitting puts 35-40% more pressure on
the intervertebral discs (cushions between the spinal
vertebrae) than does either standing or walking. This
usually leads to spasm of the lower back muscles resulting in chronic back pain. Over a long period of
time, prolonged sitting can eventually lead to a slipped
or herniated disc. These discs contain a gelatin-like
material, which under extreme pressure can actually
be squeezed out like toothpaste, resulting in what is
called a slipped disc. A recent study conducted at Yale
University found that people who sat at work more
than 6 hours daily had a 60% greater risk of developing a slipped disc than workers who walked or stood
most of the day.

Other similar studies have also found a significantly higher incidence of back problems in people
whose jobs required prolonged driving each day. Statistics show that people who spend more than two-thirds
of their day driving have a 75% higher risk of developing a slipped disc than people who stand or walk most
of the day. The cause of this high incidence resulted
from both the weight of the sitting body on the low
back and the pneumatic drill-like effect of road vibra-
tion on the spine. These two effects can eventually lead
to degeneration of the intervertebral discs.

The only way to prevent back problems from occurring is to get out of your chair and walk. If you're
desk-bound at your job, make sure you go out for a
walk at lunchtime, rather than sitting for another
hour. Make it a point to get up from your desk frequently to get a drink, go to the bathroom or just to

walk around the office. And for those who drive a lot each day, make frequent pit-stops, just to get out and stretch your legs. Remember, most of those who sat, eventually got bad backs.

SITTING TOO OFTEN PUTS YOU IN AN EARLY COFFIN

Physical inactivity is actually a double risk factor for developing coronary heart disease. First of all, inactivity is associated with obesity, hypertension, and elevated blood fats, uric acid and blood sugar. All of these factors in themselves are risk factors for developing heart disease. Secondly, epidemiological studies have demonstrated that physical inactivity by itself is a major risk factor in the development of heart disease.

These studies have also proven that physical activity, both occupational and recreational, significantly reduces the chances of developing heart disease. Those people who walk regularly also have a much better chance of surviving a heart attack should they be unfortunate enough to sustain one. Walking actually protects you from developing coronary heart disease.

Walking also helps to reduce the other coronary risk factors. Several recent studies have shown that walking may not only prevent heart disease from occurring, but it may actually reverse the changes in the coronary arteries that have already occurred in people with heart disease.

Walking accomplishes these miraculous changes by lowering the bad LDL-cholesterol and triglyceride levels in the blood. It also raises the good HDL-cholesterol which has a protective effect on the heart. Walking also decreases the blood vessel's vascular resistance thus lowering your blood pressure. It also decreases both the resting and exercise heart rates. Walking promotes weight loss and prevents the blood sugar and uric acid from getting too high, otherwise, diabetes and gout could possibly develop. Walking also helps to prevent clot formation by decreasing clot-forming agents in the blood. And, finally, walking decreases neuromuscular tension which combats anxiety and depression.

> Now if you need another reason
> Why you should walk each season
> You should know that sitting too often
> Will put you in an early coffin
> So, remember, Walk, Don't Die
> If you want to stay alive

THE WONDERFUL WORLD OF WALKING

1. Walking can be done at any time and any place, and it requires no special equipment.

2. Walking is a pleasurable exercise, and it provides a feeling of well being.

3. Walking involves no competition, thus lessening the anxiety factor and tension state.

4. Walking requires no specific athletic ability or training and above all it is the easiest type of exercise.

5. Walking is an aerobic exercise, which means that it increases the supply and distribution of oxygen throughout the body.

6. Walking provides the same cardiovascular fitness and health conditioning benefits as running or any other strenuous exercises.

7. Walking is not mentally or physically tiring and

can be done either alone, or with others—the choice is yours.

8. Walking is helpful in weight reduction and maintenance, and improves mucle tone.

9. Walking helps to improve the circulation and assists in the lowering of blood pressure.

10. Walking has been reported to lower serum lipids (fats circulating in the blood), which have been implicated in the development of heart disease.

11. Walking can be considered the only safe lifetime exercise, and is the perfect conditioner for the retirement years.

12. **No one ever died of walking!**

GET A CHECK-UP BEFORE
YOU STEP-UP

Even though walking is the safest and most hazard-free exercise known to man or woman, it is still essential that you have a complete physical examination by your family physician before starting your walking program. A thorough examination will usually include a complete physical examination, your personal and family medical history, a resting electrocardiogram, a chest x-ray, complete blood testing, a urine analysis and perhaps a pulmonary function or breathing test.

An exercise electrocardiogram may also be recommended for those over 35 years of age and for anyone younger if your physician thinks that it is indicated. This type of electrocardiogram is taken while you are walking on a treadmill and measures your heart's response to stress while you are exerting yourself. Sometimes this test is combined with an injection of dye

(Thallium scan) for a more detailed evaluation of your heart's condition. A normal exercise electrocardiogram, however, does not always completely rule out the possibility of heart disease. Your physician may feel that other heart tests, like a coronary arteriogram or an echocardiogram, may be needed if he suspects that you could have heart disease.

It is essential that you follow your own individual doctor's recommendations before beginning any exercise program including walking. Follow your doctor's recommendations after he checks you with his careful eye. And remember, *Walk, Don't Die!*

MEDICAL PRECAUTIONS FOR YOUR WALKING PROGRAM

1. Even though walking is the safest and least strenuous form of exercise, it is essential that you consult your own physician before embarking upon a walking program or any other form of exercise plan whatsoever.

2. If you have a medical disorder that requires that you take medicine or treatment of any kind (e.g., high blood pressure, arthritis, diabetes, etc.), check with your physician first before starting upon your walking program.

3. If you develop chest pain, excessive fatigue, dizziness, shortness of breath, or pain and discomfort anywhere in the body, stop your walking program and see your doctor immediately.

4. Avoid any exercise, including walking immediately after eating. Time is necessary for digestion to occur. Check Chapter 9 for the **DIETSTEP® PROGRAM**, to control your weight.

5. Walk one hour every other day or ½ hour daily for good health and maximal physical fitness.

6. Avoid walking outdoors in extremely cold or hot weather, and when the humidity is above 60%. Use the **FIT-STEP**™ **INDOOR PLAN** (Chapter 12).

7. Do not smoke. Carbon monoxide from smoking decreases the blood's supply of oxygen to the body's cells and tissues. Nicotine narrows the blood vessels, which impairs the circulation. Also, don't forget about the risks of heart disease, cancer and lung disease, which are the direct result of smoking.

8. Alcohol should be restricted since it has an adverse effect on the heart's ability to respond to exercise. Many cases of abnormal heart rhythms have been reported from the combination of alcohol and exercise.

9. Anytime you become tired, stop and rest. It is important to remember that (2) thirty minute sessions or (3) twenty minute sessions spaced throughout the day are just as effective as a walk for one continuous sixty minute period. Don't push yourself, walking should be fun, not work.

10. Your heart rate usually will not exceed 85-100 beats per minute when you are walking. A rapid heart rate is not necessary for physical fitness and good health. If you become short of breath or tired or feel your heart pounding, stop and rest; you're probably walking too fast. Remember, a walking program at any speed is beneficial for fitness and good health.

WALK SOFTLY AND CARRY A BIG STICK

1. Be alert. Be aware of your surroundings.

2. Look and listen carefully and observe who is behind and in front of you.

3. Avoid an area that is unpopulated—deserted parks, trails, streets, parking lots, open fields.

4. Vary your route and time of day that you walk. Stick to daylight hours.

5. Walk in familiar or well-populated areas. Plan your route beforehand.

6. If you feel uncomfortable in any area, turn back; follow your intuition.

7. Let someone know where and when you walk. Carry change for a phone call.

8. If possible, walk with a dog, a friend, or a stick (a walking cane or stick, an umbrella, or just a branch).

9. Ignore strangers who ask you questions or call after you.

10. Don't wear radio earphones—they prevent you from hearing traffic or people coming up behind you.

11. Stay away from areas where people may hide—bushes, parked trucks, alleyways, parking lots, etc.

12. If you are threatened or are suspicious of anyone, run into a shopping center, apartment house, crowded street or just knock on someone's door.

13. Wear a whistle on a chain or carry a pocket noise

alarm. Don't hesitate to use them even if you just suspect trouble.

14. Wear light-colored clothing, especially if walking at dawn or dusk so that you are easily seen by traffic. When clothing is wet it appears darker than when it's dry, so be careful in rainy weather.

15. Never trust a moving vehicle! They'll never give you the right-of-way. Don't argue with a car—you'll be the loser.

16. Avoid overgrown or wooded areas and dark streets.

17. Stay away from parked vehicles containing strangers.

18. If you become tired, stop and rest in a populated area (example: restaurant or a store).

19. If you're lost, call a friend or the police, never hitchhike.

20. Be bright at night. Wearing **reflective material** on clothing while walking after dark or at dusk can mean the difference between a safe walk or a trip to the hospital. Reflective strips or tape on clothing can increase visibility as much as 200 to 750 feet. According to the American Committee of Accident and Poison Prevention, this reflective material could reduce night-time pedestrian deaths by 30-40%. Be bright at night, don't risk your inner light.

**"GOLF IS SURE GOOD EXERCISE, SALLY. I'VE BUILT-UP
A WHALE OF AN APPETITE ALREADY!"**

CHAPTER 11

TRIMSTEP™: BE A LEAN, MEAN WALKING MACHINE

CAVE-PEOPLE WERE LEAN AND MEAN

The diet of prehistoric men and women protected them against heart disease, diabetes and cancer, according to a recent report in the The New England Journal of Medicine. Their diet consisted primarily of *plants and wild game* (bison, deer and horses). This diet was very low in saturated fat, sugar and salt (they consumed only 1/6 of the sodium in the typical American diet). This diet was also very rich in fiber (45 grams fiber compared to 10-15 grams in the average diet now).

Although the cave-people ate as much meat as we do, the wild game was only 4-5 percent fat compared to today's beef which is 25-30 percent fat. They also had no dairy products, processed starches or refined sugar which also limited their total sugar and fat intake. And they consumed 4-5 times the amount of vitamin C that we do because of all the plant foods they ate. We

might do well to take a tip from our prehistoric ances-
tors and stick to fruits, vegetables, whole grains and
other plant food. I think we can skip the deer, bison
and horses, don't you?

There is another important reason that these
cave-women and men stayed thin and trim. They
walked a lot more than their modern-day relatives.
Walking was a necessary part of survival, for both food
gathering and as a way to protect themselves out in
the wilds. They had to stay lean and mean.

LOOK GOOD WITH OR WITHOUT YOUR CLOTHES ON

America has terrible posture and according to recent studies adults have worse posture today than
their parents had. Adolescents nowadays slouch more,
and young athletes overdo exercises that develop hol-
low backs from muscle imbalance. Foot and leg problems and sports injuries also tend to cause poor posture.

Poor posture eventually causes many chronic
low and mid-back problems in addition to leg and
shoulder deformities and pain. To correct poor posture
you must improve muscle tone. A **walking program**
is the best exercise to develop good posture and to
prevent structural abnormalities. According to orthopedic surgeons you should walk briskly while straight-
ening the upper back and tightening the lower abdominal muscles. Remember, you must concentrate on
always maintaining good posture. Walking will develop the proper muscular tone needed to look and feel
good with or without your clothes on.

Keep your shoulders back, your head up and your
stomach in. Walk briskly taking big strides and swing
your arms vigorously. Don't be afraid to step on by
those slouching, creeping, crawling, so-called window-
shopping walkers who inhabit the sidewalks. Let's

show those lazy laggards just what a lean, mean walking machine is.

LET'S DO THE TRIMSTEP™

When you walk, don't slouch. Walk tall! The way to walk is with your head up, shoulders back, stomach in, and your chest out. Learning to walk tall comes with practice but after awhile this stance will become a natural part of your Trimstep™ walking style.

Your **stride** is the single most important aspect of your walk. There is no correct stride length. Stretch as much as you can without straining when you are walking. Thrust your legs forward briskly, swing your arms vigorously and feel your energy surge forth as you walk with the Trimstep™ stride.

Keep your **pace** steady, never push and don't try to accelerate your speed when walking. If you do get tired after a short period of time, stop and rest and then re-start again at a steady and even pace. Don't rush, just walk at a comfortable Trimstep™ pace.

Your **rhythm** of walking is a condition that will come naturally as you continue your walking program. Keep your body relaxed and your stride steady and even, and your rhythm will develop naturally. Uneven walking surfaces that you encounter will control your rhythm, especially going down or up hill. Don't fight it, just walk naturally and you'll be doing the **Trimstep™**.

TRIMSTEP™:
A FIGURE SUPREME & A BODY THAT'S LEAN

The **Trimstep™ walking plan** will shape your body beautifully. You'll never have to worry about having a pot belly, flabby thighs, sagging breasts, rounded shoulders, a curved spine, jelly upper arms, drooping chins or a protuberant posterior. By just walking a half hour a day with a brisk step (3 miles per hr) and lots of pep your body will begin to take on a new firmer shape.

Stretch your stride, swing your arms, throw back your chest, lift up your head, suck in your gut and you'll Trimstep™ like you've never walked before. Put energy into each Trimstep™ you take and your body will burn lean from this energy steam. As you burn away the pounds your body will take on its new trim shape.

The Trimstep™ body shaping plan depends on one factor only—walking briskly for one-half hour daily. There are no calories to count, no diets to follow, no starvation tactics to endure and no diet aids to depend on. Your body will automatically slim down gradually every day that you take your one-half hour brisk walk. Your figure will become trim as you lose those unsightly flabby pounds. And as you walk briskly for one-half hour daily, your muscles will tighten, firming up your figure that was hidden under all that flab.

Walking briskly every day for at least one-half hour is all the exercise you'll need to firm and shape your body beautifully. There are no strenuous calisthenics, back-breaking exercises or painful mangle machines to endure. To shape your figure all you have to do is walk at a brisk pace of 3 miles per hour with a healthy stride and a brisk arm motion. This is the only step you need for the Trimstep™ Plan to a figure supreme and a body that's lean.

You will start to develop a sprightly step as you do the Trimstep™. Your stride will become smooth and effortless as you thrust your legs forward. You will begin to develop a lively spring and bounce with every step that you take. You'll see later in this chapter how to walk with the **Trimstep™ Heel-Toe-Method.** This walking method helps to stimulate the circulation throughout the entire body.

As you do the Trimstep™ your chest will expand, providing more room for your heart and lungs to work efficiently. Your stomach muscles will tighten and suck in that unsightly gut, supporting your internal organs properly, in the fashion that they were accustomed to being supported when your abdominal muscles were in their prime.

Your posture will improve as your shoulders find their way back to their upright position. Your head will once again assume the erect position that it had when you were a young man or woman. Your back and spine will straighten like the shoot of a young branch. Your buttocks and thigh muscles will tighten and firm up, and your upper arms will lose their flabby appearance.

Your figure will slowly go through a metamorphosis and you will appear younger, feel better and be healthier than you ever were before. You will actually slow down the aging process to the point at which you will look and feel 10-15 years younger. Your weight will decrease to its teen-age level as you travel the Trimstep™ program. You will burn steam as your energy beam keeps you lean with a figure supreme.

Walk off weight, walk off worry, walk off stress and tension as you walk away the years and the ravages of aging. The Trimstep™ program will give you a perfect "10" body as you feel and look younger and younger and younger. You'll hear your friends and neighbors say—"Boy, I didn't know his wife was so young," or "When did he re-marry that young girl," or "She looks young enough to be his daughter." And when they get up close they'll say, "My God, I didn't recognize you. Did you have a face-lift or a body tuck or something?" And you'll just say, "No, I just do the Trimstep™." And of course they'll say, "What's that?" And you'll say, "I really can't go into it now; I have a rather important appointment." As you walk away, they'll say, "Who does she think she's fooling. She had a face lift and probably a body lift for that matter. Now will you look at that, she even walks differently!"

I guarantee you a better figure, a leaner body and a younger you, when you do the Trimstep™. Don't give in to the ravages of the aging process which cause spineless jelly figures of men and women. Don't let inactivity sap your bones of their calcium, your muscles of their strength and your body of its life. Don't let your body start to sag before its time. Use your only defense available against the aging process—walking every day the Trimstep™ way—towards a **figure supreme** and a **body that's lean.**

YOUR VERY OWN
ROLLS ROYCE MACHINE

We are structurally built for walking, but not for running. Since the runner pounds the ground with a force equal to three to four times his body weight, he is more likely to sustain injuries than the walker. Walking is one of the most natural functions of the human body. Due to the structure of our musculo-skeletal system and the shape and flexibility of our spine, our bodies are perfectly constructed for walking.

As we walk the muscular and skeletal systems perform synchronously together. Our curved flexible spine has a spring-like function, made up of many vertebrae, each separated from the other by a tiny cushion (intervertebral-disc) which is designed to absorb shock. These discs also give the spine its resilience and flexibility. When we walk we use the hinge-like joints in our feet, ankles and knees while the ball and socket joints in our hips move effortlessly with a fluid-like motion.

Your muscles that are attached to the long bones of the legs and the pelvis are specifically designed for walking. The leg, hip and back muscles are used for support and the mechanics of propelling the body forward. The long bones of your legs form a framework of levers which are moved by these muscles, and subsequently help to propel the body forward. Your abdominal muscles support the weight of your abdominal organs when you walk and your chest wall and diaphragm muscles assist in respiration.

As your legs thrust forward, you are in effect catching the forward motion of the upper part of your body. This natural motion in walking creates a perfect balance between gravity's force and the forward thrust of your body. The act of walking is therefore an almost effortless bio-dynamic mechanism, structurally more efficient than any man-made machine, even a Rolls Royce.

BE LEAN! BE MEAN!
BE A WALKING MACHINE

Walking produces a remarkable number of changes that occur inside of your body. Your *blood volume* increases and the *red blood cells* increase in number. Your *heart* pumps blood more efficiently. Your *lungs* expand, taking in and distributing more oxygen. Your *muscles* tighten and contract giving you a firmer figure. Your *energy* level increases, and you feel strong and fit. The results of these changes will make your figure lean and mean and your posture supreme.

Your overall appearance will improve following your daily walk, since walking will improve your *circulation* and enable you to feel and look great. Your skin complexion and hair texture will also improve with walking because of the increased blood circulation to the skin and hair follicles. Your complexion will literally glow after your walk and your skin will stay healthy and fresh looking all day long.

After you have been walking for a while you will notice that your muscles will become firm and many of the fatty deposits on your thighs and buttocks will start to decrease in size. Your *stomach* will become flatter and the muscles of your *calves, thighs* and *buttocks* will become firmer. These changes result from improved muscle tone and also from the strengthening of muscles and ligaments which are attached to the spine.

You don't have to kill yourself to stay fit, trim and healthy. Walking actually provides better long-term figure control and fitness benefits than jogging or other strenuous exercises, without the hazards and dangers. Always remember that exercise does not have to be painful or uncomfortable to be effective. The **Trimstep**™ walking plan provides the easy steps needed for a trim, beautiful body. *Be lean! Be mean! Be a walking machine!*

DON'T LET YOUR
MACHINERY RUST

The **Trimstep**™ walking method is the ideal weight control and fitness program. Studies in human physiology have proven that walking acts as a weight reduction plan without actually dieting and a fitness program without strenuous exercises. Too often today we allow a sedentary lifestyle to dominate our daily living. We sit at our desks all day and in front of the TV set in the evenings. We drive to our destination, no matter how close or how far, instead of doing what's easy, natural and healthful—walking.

Most of us would rather spend 15 minutes in our cars waiting at the drive-in window of a bank, rather than getting out and walking the length of the parking lot. Even at golf we follow the easy path. Instead of using and enjoying this healthful and relaxing sport in a positive way for fitness and exercise, we allow ourselves to be "driven" in little motorized carts around the course. You might as well stay at home and watch golf on TV.

In order to lose and control weight effectively, the

energy burned during exercise should come from body fats rather than from carbohydrates. As we have previously seen, we burn more body fat after long periods of a sustained activity (walking) than we do after brief bouts of strenuous exercise (jogging). It is therefore apparent that walking is far superior to brief flurries of exercise for a complete and effective weight reduction and weight control program. The beauty of a walking program is that you can stay fit, trim and healthy as long as you don't let your walking machinery rust.

Our bodies are one of the few machines that break down when not in use. A physically active person is one who is both physically and mentally alert. A walking program can actually slow down the aging process and add years to our lives. Walking has been proven to be a significant factor in the prevention of heart and vascular disease. It strengthens the heart muscle, improves the lungs' efficiency and lowers the blood pressure by keeping the blood vessels flexible. Walking will add years to your life, and life to your years!

THE TRIMSTEP™ PLAN KEEPS YOUR BODY LEAN AND YOUR ARTERIES CLEAN

In order to walk comfortably and efficiently without tiring, you should balance your body weight over the feet or just slightly ahead of them. Keep your body relaxed, and your knees bent slightly, utilizing a steady, even pace, and a brisk walking stride. To obtain the most benefit out of your walking program, it is essential to walk with the **Trimstep™ heel-and-toe method**, pointing your feet straight ahead. By utilizing this method, your leg muscles are used more efficiently, and this results in an overall increased blood supply to the peripheral circulation (in particular the legs and feet). This walking method is especially helpful in the treatment of poor circulation to the legs (Fig. 3).

The leading leg is brought forward in front of the body, thus enabling the heel of the lead foot to touch the ground just before the ball of the foot and the toes. Your weight is then shifted forward so that when your heel is raised your toes will push off for the next step. Your arms and shoulders should be relaxed, and they will swing automatically with each stride you take. Before long you will develop a natural rhythm, pace and stride as you walk. Remember to walk with the **Trimstep™ heel-and-toe method** (Fig. 3). This uses the calf muscles productively to pump the blood up through the leg veins, back to the heart and lungs, and then out through the arteries to all of your body's cells, tissues and organs. This walking method keeps your *body lean* and your *arteries clean.*

AMERICANS ARE DOING THE TRIMSTEP™

A recent Gallup Poll sponsored by American Health Magazine showed that approximately 54 percent of Americans exercise regularly. Walking was the type of exercise that 3 out of 5 people engaged in most often. Almost 50 percent of those questioned said that they were walking for their health, 30 percent exercised to stay in shape, and approximately 20 percent stated that it was to lose or control weight.

This survey showed that Americans are walking again and are feeling better. The responses given for choosing walking as their favorite exercise were "easy, safe, comfortable, not too strenuous, beneficial and an exercise that you can continue for a lifetime."

Let's get out there and start walking again as if our lives depended on it. They probably do! Put life into each step and walking will repay you tenfold by putting extra years into your life. When you use your Trimstep™ walking machine, you don't have to really be mean to stay lean, but you know what I mean.

FIGURE 3

DON'T BE A HEEL, SAID THE TOE

To get the most out of your walking program, walk with the Trimstep™ heel-and-toe method. Proper walking uses calf muscles more productively and improves blood flow to these muscles. The diagram below explains heel-and-toe walking.

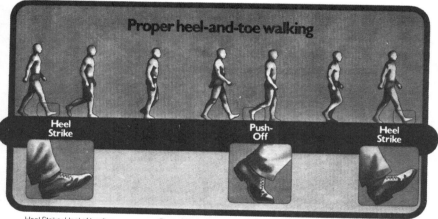

Proper heel-and-toe walking

| Heel Strike | Push-Off | Heel Strike |

Heel Strike: Heel of leading foot touches the floor before the ball of the foot and toes

Push-Off: Knee is bent so heel is raised; weight is shifted forward. (This is essential and you should feel the action in the calf muscles.) Toes push off to next step.

Heel Strike: Leg is accelerated forward to get in front of body. Foot is positioned for next heel strike

With permission of U.S.V. Laboratories, Inc., Medical Dept., Tuckahoe, N.Y.

GIVE YOUR FEET A TREAT

Proper foot care is essential to any exercise program since the feet are vulnerable to injury and disease. The foot is a very complex structure consisting of 26 bones, 56 ligaments and 38 muscles. The feet not only carry the entire weight of the body, but they are essential in holding the body in an upright position and maintaining the body's balance during walking. Since your feet are the parts of the body that are located furthest from your heart, their circulation generally tends to be decreased, especially as you get older.

Constant pounding on hard surfaces causes the feet to absorb considerable shock and consequently subjects them to injury. The feet are also prone to the growth of fungi and bacteria because of the moist warm climate created by shoes and socks. These factors all point to the necessity of proper foot care in your Trimstep™ walking program.

FOOT FACTS FOR FEET

1. Avoid the use of **tight-fitting garments**, including stockings, socks and garters, which can reduce the circulation to the lower extremities.

2. Avoid **prolonged sitting**, especially with your legs crossed, as this can also reduce the blood supply to your legs.

3. If you develop a cramping pain in your legs and feet while you're walking, which is relieved by rest and resumes again upon walking, see your doctor at once. You may have **poor circulation** in your legs. This can be caused by a narrowing of the arteries, preventing blood from reaching your legs and feet.

4. Dress sensibly since extremes in **temperature** can impair the circulation in the legs.

5. **Nicotine** constricts (narrows) the blood vessels and can result in impaired circulation. Smoking also causes a build-up of carbon monoxide in your blood and a decrease in the amount of oxygen carried to your legs.

6. **Exercise your feet** daily without shoes by walking barefoot on a carpet and flex your toes up and down any time you take off your shoes.

7. Keep feet **clean and dry**, especially between toes. Wash with deodorant soap and dry carefully. Use foot powder when necessary.

8. **Clean soft, loose-fitting stockings and socks** prevent odor forming bacteria and sweat from building up. They also help to prevent the formation of blisters and calluses.

9. **Cut nails** straight across, never down in the grooves on the sides of your toes.

10. **Dry scaly feet**—use moisturizing lotion. Cracking or redness between the toes may be caused by a fungus. Check with your doctor.

11. **Tired, aching feet**—treat to a warm water soak after walking, dry thoroughly.

12. **Foot problems:** corns, bunions, calluses, blisters, ingrown toenails, sores, ulcers, cracks, pain or swelling should be reported to your doctor.

13. **Walk, don't run**, and your feet will still be able to have fun.

TRIMSTEP™ INTO THE BEST SHOE FOR YOU

1. Wear a *properly fitted,* low-heeled shoe for maximum comfort and safety. Remember, make sure the shoe fits, no matter what the style. Shoes should be at least 1/2-3/4 of an inch longer than your longest toe.

2. The *toe-section* should be wide and high enough so as not to cause compression of the toes.

3. The *shank* (section between heel and ball of foot) should be wide enough to fit the bottom of your foot comfortably.

4. The *uppers* (part of the shoe above the sole) should be soft and flexible enough to bend with your foot, such as soft leather, fabrics and suedes. Avoid synthetic materials (man made) such as vinyl and patent leather since they are not porous or flexible.

5. The *sole and heel* of the shoe should preferably be made of a thick resilient material (foam rubber or crepe). These are the most practical for every day use, since they are the most durable. Well-cushioned soles are extremely comfortable and give resiliency to your step, thus absorbing some of the shock encountered when walking on a hard surface. They also lessen your chance of slipping.

6. *Sneakers* or *running shoes* should only be worn if they have a wide, high, flexible toe box. This allows enough space to prevent crowding of the toes, which can result in toe and nail injuries. Most of them however, do not provide good support or adequate cushioning. Many of them also cause blisters and foot infections because of inadequate ventilation.

7 *High heels* cause the whole foot to slide forward, making the formation of corns, bunions, calluses and occasionally hammertoes more likely. Also continual use of high heels can actually shorten the Achilles tendon making it more susceptible to injury. They also prevent the foot from acting as a natural shock absorber and this leads to ligament strain in the foot and leg and recurrent backaches.

8. Avoid the use of *boots* with extremely high heels, since they interfere with your balance. These boots may also cut off the circulation and cause inflammation of the calf leg veins (phlebitis).

9. Avoid high *platform shoes* and *clogs*. These shoes often lead to ankle and foot injuries, and may cause painful bleeding under the toenails.

10. *Hiking shoes* or *boots* are cumbersome and are usually not necessary unless you plan to hike over rough terrain.

11. *Flat shoes* may actually strain a woman's calf muscles since most women usually have tight calf muscles to begin with.

12. *Shoes with 1 to 2 inch heels* are the best type for walking since they help to relax the leg muscles by removing tension on the tendons and ligaments.

13. *Shoes usually smell,* not your feet. Foot odor is caused by bacteria on the shoe leather which absorbs sweat from your feet. Give shoes time to air out. If however, you find that it's your feet and not your shoes that smell, check with your doctor. You may have a bacterial or fungal foot infection.

THE IDEAL WALKING SHOE
"The Body Shoe®, by Hush Puppies® Shoes"

After many, many years of walking and several dozen pairs of walking shoes, I have finally found the *"ideal walking shoe"*—The Body Shoe®, by Hush Puppies® Shoes. These shoes come in several styles, two of which are the Challenger pattern and the Walker pattern.

1. The last is contoured on the bottom like the sole of your foot. Ordinary shoe lasts are flat.

2. The upper is cut from leather and topped with a padded collar.

3. Between two inner soles is a pad of foam extending from the ball of the foot to the heel, acting as a support and a shock absorber. This pad of foam is made of a special material called *"Memory Foam"*. This is a slow recovery, temperature sensitive foam that has been used in the medical industry in wheelchair pads, bed mattress toppers, body padding and other areas where long term comfort is a necessity. In these cases, Memory Foam has helped to prevent the formation of skin ulcers and irritation.

4. When walking, the combination of body heat and pressure causes Memory Foam to uniformly conform to the shape of the foot against it. This allows for more load spreading and reduces severe pressure points. The reduction of pressure points and more even load spreading allows blood to flow more readily into the small capillaries of the feet, thus improving the circulation.

5. A pigskin mud guard around the base of the shoe is present in the Challenger pattern and the Walker pattern features a full pigskin leather upper. Pig-

skin is a naturally soft and supple leather that breathes. Unlike cowhide, after pigskin is tanned it has tiny pores that allows fresh air in and hot, moist air out with every step. The pigskin upper on both shoes is Scotchgard® treated.

6. The inner sole nearest the foot is made of leather in the Challenger pattern. In the Walker pattern the lining is made of a new material called *Cambrelle®*. This unique material actually pulls moisture away from the foot through one-way pores in the fabric so that it can dissipate naturally through the leather uppers.

7. The outer sole is made of urethane. The layer nearest the foot is soft to absorb shock. The bottom layer is dense and very tough to resist wear.

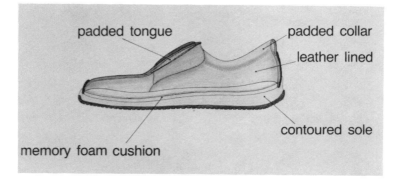

. **"The Body Shoe® by Hush Puppies® Shoes"—Wolverine World Wide, Inc.**

The Body Shoe® by Hush Puppies® Shoes—Wolverine World Wide, Inc.

CHAPTER 12

FIT-STEP™: FOR ENERGY, FITNESS AND PEP

ON YOUR MARK, GET SET, DO THE FIT-STEP™

When you first start your Fit-Step™ walking program, pick a level terrain, since hills place too much strain and stress on your legs, hips, and back muscles. Concentrate on maintaining **erect posture** while walking. Walk with your shoulders relaxed and your arms carried in a relatively low position with natural motion at the elbow. Don't hold your arms too high when you walk, otherwise you will develop muscle spasms and pain in your neck, back and shoulder muscles.

Make sure you walk at a **brisk pace** (approximately 3 mph) for maximum efficiency. When you begin walking your respirations and heart rate will automatically become faster; however, if you feel short of breath or tired, then you're probably walking too fast. Remember to stop whenever you are tired or fatigued and then resume walking after resting.

Concentrate on walking naturally, putting **energy** into each step. Soon you will begin to feel relaxed and comfortable as your **stride** becomes smooth and effortless. Walk with an even steady **gait** and your own rhythm of walking will automatically develop into an unconscious synchronous movement.

Your Fit-Step™ walking program should be planned to meet your individual schedule; however, when you begin it's a good idea to walk at a specific time every day to ensure regularity and consistency. You will be able to vary your schedule, once you have started the program. Lunchtime, for example, is an ideal time to plan a half-hour walk since it combines both calorie burning and calorie reduction. If you have less time for lunch, you'll eat less. Better yet, take an hour walk on your break and carry your lunch (example: an apple and a fruit drink or a small carton of skim milk).

TAKE THAT FIRST STEP FOR ENERGY, FITNESS AND PEP

With the advent of modern technology, man is forced by design to do less and less physical labor, since he has invented machines which do these jobs for him. It would seem that this would result in more energy available for other activities. How many times have you noticed that the less you do, the more tired you feel, whereas the more active you are, the more energy you have for other activities? Exercise improves the efficiency of the lungs, the heart and the circulatory system in their ability to take in and deliver *oxygen* throughout the entire body. This oxygen is the catalyst which burns the fuel (food) we take in to produce energy. Consequently, the more oxygen we take in, the more *energy* we have for all of our activities.

Oxygen is the vital ingredient which is necessary for our survival. Since oxygen can't be stored, our cells need a continuous supply in order to remain healthy. Walking increases your body's ability to extract oxygen from the air, so that increased amounts of oxygen are available for every organ, tissue and cell in the body. Walking actually increases the *total volume of blood,* making more red blood cells available to carry oxygen and nutrition to the tissues, and to remove carbon dioxide and waste products from the body's cells. This increased saturation of the tissues with oxygen is also aided by the opening of *small blood vessels,* which is another direct result of walking.

So let's take that first step for energy, fitness and pep. Walking every day will keep a fresh supply of oxygen surging through your blood vessels to all of your body's hungry cells. Don't disappoint these little fellows because you depend on them as much as they depend on you. If you short-change them on their daily oxygen supply, they'll take it out on you in the form of illness and disease. A Fit-Step™ a day keeps the doctor away.

FIT-STEP™:
4-WEEKS IS ALL YOU NEED

To get the most benefit from your Fit-Step™ walking program, you should walk **one hour every other day** or **½ hour daily** after you have completed the **4-week Fit-Step™ conditioning program** (Table III). The following table includes the slow, brisk and fast pace schedules for the first four weeks of your Fit-Step™ program. It is not important which pace you choose as long as you are comfortable with it and consistent in the **TIME** that you walk every other day. In fact, you may find that your pace (miles per hour) falls somewhere in between any of these walking speeds. This is perfectly acceptable, since this program of walking is based on *regularity* and *consistency—*

NOT SPEED. Remember, the Fit-Step™ program is for good health and fitness, not for speed records.

Once you have completed this 4-week conditioning program, you are ready to begin walking ½ **hour daily** or **1 hour every other day of the week**. How far should you walk in this hour? Don't worry. It's the **time**, and not the distance, which is the most important factor. Whether you walk 2, 2½, 3 or even 4 miles in *one hour*, you will still gain the same fitness, health and weight loss benefits from your Fit-Step™ walking program.

Remember, the speed of walking is not important, unless you are walking too slowly (under 2 mph). The

TABLE III

YOUR 4-WEEK FIT-STEP™ CONDITIONING PROGRAM

WEEK/DAY	TIME	SLOW PACE (2 mph) DISTANCE	BRISK PACE (3 mph) DISTANCE	FAST PACE (4 mph) DISTANCE
1st Mon.	15 min.	½ mile	¾ mile	1 mile
1st Wed.	15 min.	½ mile	¾ mile	1 mile
1st Fri.	15 min.	½ mile	¾ mile	1 mile
1st Sun.	15 min.	½ mile	¾ mile	1 mile
2nd Mon.	30 min.	1 mile	1½ miles	2 miles
2nd Wed.	30 min.	1 mile	1½ miles	2 miles
2nd Fri.	30 min.	1 mile	1½ miles	2 miles
2nd Sun.	30 min.	1 mile	1½ miles	2 miles
3rd Mon.	45 min.	1½ miles	2¼ miles	3 miles
3rd Wed.	45 min.	1½ miles	2¼ miles	3 miles
3rd Fri.	45 min.	1½ miles	2¼ miles	3 miles
3rd Sun.	45 min.	1½ miles	2¼ miles	3 miles
4th Mon.	60 min.	2 miles	3 miles	4 miles
4th Wed.	60 min.	2 miles	3 miles	4 miles
4th Fri.	60 min.	2 miles	3 miles	4 miles
4th Sun.	60 min.	2 miles	3 miles	4 miles

most important factor is that you walk regularly at a relatively brisk pace. If you become tired easily or get short of breath then you are probably walking too fast (4 mph is usually too strenuous for most of us). If these symptoms persist or any other unusual symptoms occur, check with your physician. See Medical Precautions—Chapter 10.

HOW MANY STEPS IN THE FIT-STEP™?

Remember, it's the the amount of **TIME** that you walk every day that is more important than the distance or even the speed. If you walk **1 hour every other day** or ½ **hour every day**, it doesn't make any difference whether you are walking 2, 2½, or 3 miles per hour. You are still burning calories, losing weight, and developing physical fitness. In other words, **it does not matter how far you walk as long as you walk regularly**.

If you would like to measure how far you've walked, the simplest way is to use the odometer on your car. Drive along the course you intend to walk and the odometer will record the distance you traveled in miles. Once having done this a few times you will be able to measure similar distances in the same neighborhood or area by yourself. Ten to twelve city blocks usually equals one mile, so that if you walk around one square block approximately three times, you will have walked approximately one mile.

There are other more specific methods of measuring distance which we will now discuss. Remember, however, that these methods are for your own information and pleasure in walking. They are not a necessary part of your Fit-Step™ walking program since it is only the **TIME** that you walk each day, and not the distance which is really important.

1. FIT-STEP™ PEDOMETER

By far the easiest method for measuring distance is using a pedometer. For a nominal fee, you can purchase a reliable pedometer at any sporting goods store. It is a small instrument resembling a watch, which attaches to your belt or pocket, and measures how far you walk in any given time period. Its mechanism depends upon an oscillating weight which causes the dial to advance a certain distance with each step. All you have to do is set the stride-length adjustment on the pedometer and walk at a steady even pace. The distance you walk in any given time period is then recorded on the dial.

2. FIT-STEP™ WALKING SPEEDS (mph)

Another easy method you can use for estimating the distance that you walk is to actually time your walk. This method is based on the most common walking speeds (measured in miles per hour): slow (2 mph), brisk (3 mph), and fast (4 mph).

DISTANCE	SLOW SPEED 2 mph	BRISK SPEED 3 mph	FAST SPEED 4 mph
½ mile	15 minutes	10 minutes	7½ minutes
1 mile	30 minutes	20 minutes	15 minutes
1½ miles	45 minutes	30 minutes	22½ minutes
2 miles	60 minutes	40 minutes	30 minutes
2½ miles	75 minutes	50 minutes	37½ minutes
3 miles	90 minutes	60 minutes	45 minutes

Example: Take a 30 minute walk in an area that is familiar to you. Consult the chart. If you have walked 1 mile, then you walk at a speed of 2 mph. If you've covered a distance of 1½ miles, then your walking speed is 3 mph. And if you've walked a distance of 2 miles in 30 minutes, your walking speed is 4 mph (probably too fast). After you become sure of your walking speed (Ex.: 3 mph), you can estimate how far you've walked in areas where you are unfamiliar with distances. Time your walk, consult the chart under the column of your walking speed and you'll see just how far you've walked.

3. FIT-STEP™ STEPS

You can also determine the time it takes you to walk one mile by counting the number of steps that you take in one minute at your normal walking speed. The following chart is based upon the average stride, which is approximately *two feet per step*. Since there are 5,280 feet in one mile, and you divide that by 2 feet, then it it will take 2,640 steps to walk one mile. Refer to the step/min. column in the following chart, and find the number closest to the number of steps you take per minute. You will then have the approximate time it will take you to walk one mile. For example, if you take about 90 steps per minute, then it will take you approximately 30 minutes to walk a mile or 60 minutes to walk two miles; therefore you walk at a speed of 2 mph. Sound complicated? It is!

STEPS/MILE (2 foot stride)	STEPS/MINUTE	DISTANCE WALKED	TIME
2,640	44	1 mile	60 minutes
2,640	48	1 mile	55 minutes
2,640	53	1 mile	50 minutes
2,640	59	1 mile	45 minutes
2,640	66	1 mile	40 minutes
2,640	75	1 mile	35 minutes
2,640	88	1 mile	30 minutes
2,640	106	1 mile	25 minutes
2,640	132	1 mile	20 minutes
2,640	176	1 mile	15 minutes

Note: This chart will vary slightly depending upon the length of your foot and the length of your stride. To determine your stride length in feet, measure the distance from toe to toe or heel to heel that you take with each step. If your stride is more or less than two feet, then you have to divide that number into 5,280 feet and make up a new chart. If you want my advice, you'll forget this chart entirely and go out and take a nice refreshing Fit-Step™ walk.

TAKE THE NEXT STEP FOR VIGOR, VIM AND PEP

At the end of your 4-week Fit-Step™ conditioning program you will begin to notice the many changes brought about by your improved **aerobic fitness and maximum oxygen capacity** (the uptake and distribution of oxygen through your body). You will have lots of pep and energy, a trim figure, improved breathing capacity and muscle tone, improved exercise tolerance, a better night's sleep, a feeling of peace and relaxation, and a lessening of tension. Once you have completed this 4-week conditioning program, you will have taken the first steps towards improved cardiovascular fitness, good health and a long, happy life.

The great part about walking as an exercise, is that you aren't limited to a particular time or location. Walking doesn't require special clothes, shoes or equipment. You can walk before or after work or if you drive to work, you can park your car a block or two from the office, and walk the rest of the way. If you take the bus or train, get off a stop before your station and walk. An enclosed mall could be the perfect place for your walk in bad weather. Remember to take that half hour from your lunch break and walk, or just walk for the whole hour. Just think of how good that fresh air will feel.

Each city usually has a guide book containing historical sites, restaurants, shops of interest, cultural centers, and interesting walking tours. If you live near a park, the country or the seashore, a walking trip will be a refreshing change. Take the time to walk everywhere. Each new area has its own natural beauty. The wonderful world of walking is literally at your feet. For more information about the highways and byways of walking, check the Fit-Step™ Walking and Hiking Organizations at the end of this chapter. Just take that next step for *vigor, vim* and *pep.*

THE INDOOR FIT-STEP™— NOT JUST ANOTHER TRENDY DANCE

Don't wait until the "weather is better" to go out and walk. There's no excuse for not exercising at home on any day when the weather is too bad to go outdoors. Be careful about walking when the weather is too cold or windy. Also take precautions against exercising when it's very hot or humid outdoors. Heat exhaustion and occasionally heat stroke are complications frequently found in those crazy screwball jogging nuts that you see running on hot humid days. Remember it's not necessary to walk outdoors if the weather is extremely cold, windy, wet, hot or humid. Here are a few ways to stay on your **FIT-STEP™ Program**:

1. STATIONARY FIT-STEP™:

This is a combination of walking and running in place. Walk in place for 5 minutes lifting your foot approximately 4 inches off the floor and taking approximately 60 steps a minute (count only when right foot hits floor).

Alternate this with 5 minutes of running in place lifting your foot approximately 8 inches off the floor and taking approximately

90 steps a minute (again only count when the right foot hits the floor).

Use a padded exercise mat or a thick rug. Wear a padded sneaker or walking shoe. Bare feet will cause foot and leg injuries. Repeat this walk-run cycle (10 minutes total) 2 or 3 times daily. If you tire easily, stop and rest.

2. TV FIT-STEP™:

If you have a large family room or a basement recreation room, you can set up 2 TV sets at opposite ends of the room. You can walk for ¼ hour twice a day while watching your favorite shows. You can even watch two different shows at the same time as you walk in one direction and then the other. If you only have one TV, then you can watch when walking towards the TV and listen when walking away from the set. It may look silly, but so are the programs on TV.

3. SKIPPING FIT-STEP™:

If you're coordinated enough to use a rope, skipping can be a fun indoor exercise. Skip over the rope alternating one foot at a time for 5 minutes and then skip using both feet together for 5 minutes. Use a mat or padded rug with a padded low sneaker or walking shoe.

This 10 minute session can be repeated 3 times daily. If you feel that you are not coordinated enough for rope skipping, then *skip it!*

4. STAIR FIT-STEP™:

A rather boring but effective method for aerobic fitness is walking up and down the stairs—not running. Wear a padded sneaker or a padded walking shoe and hold on to the rail on your way up and down. This is the only indoor exercise so far that you can't watch TV with.

Five minutes 3 times daily should be more than enough if you can stand it or rather step it. Walk at a speed that is comfortable for you.

5. STATIONARY BIKE FIT-STEP™

One of the easiest ways to continue your indoor Fit-Step™ program is by using a stationary exercise bicycle. This is the only one-time investment you'll ever need to make as you travel the road towards fitness and good health. No other type of exercise equipment is necessary for your Fit-Step™ program. Beware of the **mangle machines** (see Chapter 5).

The most important features to look for in a stationary bicycle are a comfortable seat with good support, adjustable handle bars, a chain guard, a quiet pedal and chain, and a solid front wheel. Most come with speedometers to tell the rate that you are pedaling and odometers to tell the mileage that you pedal. An inexpensive stationary bike works just as well as an expensive one.

Stationary bikes with moving handle bars are worthless. They claim to exercise the upper half of your body. In reality, they move your arms and back muscles passively, which can result in pulled muscles and strained ligaments.

The stationary bike is the safest and most efficient type of indoor exercise equipment that can be used in place of your outdoor walking program. You can listen to music, watch TV, talk on the telephone, or even read (a bookstand attachment can easily be clamped onto the handle bars) while riding your stationary bike. If the bike comes with a tension dial, leave it on zero or minimal tension. Remember, it is not necessary to strain yourself to develop aerobic fitness. Exercises like walking and the stationary bike can be fun, without being painful or stressful.

You should pedal at a comfortable rate of approximately **15 miles/ hour**. This will complete your daily exercise requirements in **30 minutes** (divided into three 10-minute sessions or two 15 minute sessions to avoid fatigue). Consult the following table for the 5-week stationary Fit-Step™ bike-conditioning program before you begin (Table IV).

* * *

CAUTION: If any of these Fit-Step™ indoor exercises cause excessive fatigue, weakness, shortness of breath, dizziness, headaches, chest pain, pain anywhere in the body or any other unusual symptoms or signs, stop immediately and consult your physician. See Medical Precautions—Chapter 10.

TABLE IV
5 WEEK FIT-STEP™ CONDITIONING PROGRAM
FOR STATIONARY BIKES WITH SPEEDOMETERS
AND ODOMETERS

WEEKS	TOTAL TIME PER DAY (MIN/SEC)	DIVIDED INTO 3 SESSIONS OF (MIN/SEC)	DISTANCE TOTAL (MILES)	SPEED (MPH)	FREQUENCY (DAYS) PER WEEK
1	10:00	3:20	2 1/2	15	4
2	15:00	5:00	3 3/4	15	4
3	20:00	6:40	5	15	4
4	25:00	8:20	6 1/4	15	4
5	30:00	10:00	7 1/2	15	4

MAINTENANCE SCHEDULE

30:00 min	10:00 min	7½ miles	15 mph	4 days/wk

NOTES:

1. Get a complete physical exam from your physician before using the stationary bike. Check Medical Precautions (Chapter 10).

2. Time pedaled and miles per hour are only approximate. If 15 miles per hour is too fast—slow down.

3. Stop at the first indication of palpitations, weakness, fatigue, shortness of breath, dizziness or pain and/or discomfort anywhere. Always check with your doctor if any unusual symptoms occur.

4. Follow conditioning chart for good health and physical fitness. Do not attempt to set endurance or speed records.

5. The above table can be used to supplement, or replace your outdoor Fit-Step™ walking program, depending on weather.

6. If you are already finished with your 4-week outdoor Fit-Step™ conditioning walking program (**TABLE III**), you may be able to follow the daily maintenance schedule without going through the stationary bike conditioning program. If you get tired, move back a week or two.

7. If you have not completed your 4-week outdoor Fit-Step™ conditioning program, use common sense and your own level of physical fitness to determine which week you will begin with on the above table. It's best to start at the beginning.

8. You may alternate days of outdoor walking and indoor cycling or you may even divide each day into half outdoor and half indoor exercise. The choice is yours.

9. Wear a walking shoe or sneaker (never pedal barefoot). A chain guard prevents clothing from getting caught in bike chain; otherwise roll up trousers.

10. Don't exercise immediately after a meal, before bedtime or when you are feeling ill. Always make sure the room has proper ventilation.

TRAVEL FIT WITH THE FIT-STEP™

Whether you're taking a vacation or a business trip, you can still keep trim and fit with your walking program. Most major airlines, cruise ships and trains offer special diet menus. If you have to splurge on one meal a day, don't worry. You'll walk it off in no time at all.

Cruise ships and trains are ideal for short walks. Walk around the airport concourse while waiting for flights or during layovers. Most major *hotels* can give you a map of the area for a walking tour. Get up early before your meeting and take a brisk ½ hour walk and repeat it again before supper. Use the *stairs* whenever possible and walk around the hotel as much as possible if the weather is bad.

Many hotels have small *gyms* where you can swim or use a stationary bike—take advantage of them if the weather's bad instead of watching TV. Many business trips are associated with a lot of stress and walking can ease away the tension leaving you more relaxed and more efficient. Speakers always do better after they've had a walk—more brain oxygen and relaxing chemicals (endorphins) and less carbon dioxide results in a sharp, clear, concise speech with no stage jitters.

You can keep fit and have lots of pep when you do the **FIT-STEP™**. Don't let a little trip, trip you up. Most people feel exhausted after a vacation or a business trip because they sit around all day and stuff their faces with food and drink. Make it a habit to walk at least ½ hour every day that you're away. You'll return from your travels fit, full of vigor, vim and pep.

FIT-STEP™
WALKING AND HIKING
ORGANIZATIONS

Adirondac Mountain Club, Inc.
172 Ridge Street
Glen Falls, NY 12801

American Forestry Association
1319 18th Street, N.W.
Washington, DC 20036

American Hiking Society
1701 18th Street, N.W.
Washington, DC 20009

American Youth Hostels
75 Spring Street
New York, NY 10012

Appalachian Mountain Club
5 Joy Street
Boston, MA 02108

Appalachian Trail Conference
P.O. Box 236
Harpers Ferry, WV 25425

Dietwalk® Association of
   America
3501 Newberry Road
Philadelphia, PA 19154

The Federation of Western
   Outdoor Clubs
512½ Boylston E. #106
Seattle, WA 98102

National Audubon Society
950 Third Avenue
New York, NY 10022

National Campers & Hikers
   Association
7172 Transit Road
Buffalo, NY 14221

National Park Service
North Atlantic Regional Office
15 State Street
Boston, MA 02109

National Wildlife Federation
1412 16th Street, N.W.
Washington, DC 20036

The New England Trail
   Conference
P.O. Box 115
West Pawlet, VT 05775

Potomac Appalachian Trail Club
1718 N. Street, N.W.
Washington, DC 20036

Sierra Club
530 Bush Street
San Francisco, CA 94108

U.S. Forest Service
Box 3623
Information Office
Portland, OR 97208

U.S. Geological Survey
(Areas West of Mississippi)
P.O. Box 25286
Federal Center
Denver, CO 80225

U.S. Geological Survey
(Areas East of Mississippi)
1200 S. Eads Street
Arlington, VA 22202

Walkabout International
Box 6540
San Diego, CA 92106

Walking Association
4113 Lee Highway
Arlington, VA 22207

Wilderness Society
1901 Pennsylvania Avenue,
    N.W.
Washington, DC 20036

**"LIFE IS WONDERFUL, LIFE IS SWEET. IF YOU WANT TO
PROLONG IT, MOVE YOUR FEET!"**

V. WALK, DON'T DIE

"Walking every day is one of the only defenses that we have against the degenerative diseases of aging. Walking controls weight, lowers blood pressure, reduces stress and tension, retards cancer, prevents heart disease and strokes, and slows the aging process. If you want to live an additional 15, 20, even 25 years, then you'd better start walking as if your life depended on it—It does!"

—Fred A. Stutman, M.D.
"The Today Show," NBC, July 1980

"NOW HARRY, WHEN I TOLD YOU TO WALK EVERY DAY, I DIDN'T MEAN JUST FROM THE TV TO THE REFRIGERATOR!"

CHAPTER 13

HEARTSTEP: LIVE LONGER WITHOUT BYPASS SURGERY

HEART DISEASE

Coronary heart disease is responsible for over one-half million deaths each year in the United States. It causes more deaths each year than all forms of cancer combined. There are over 5½ million Americans who have been diagnosed as having coronary artery disease. It is estimated that there are at least 2½ million other Americans with undiagnosed coronary heart disease, many of them under the age of 50.

Coronary artery disease is caused by the build-up of fat deposits in the arteries (atherosclerosis). This disease begins slowly, early in life, and usually doesn't produce symptoms until middle age. Unfortunately, this condition often goes undetected until the person has his/her first heart attack, which may in fact be fatal. Although we have made great strides in the treatment of heart attacks, the emphasis must rest on preventing this slowly progressive disease (atherosclerosis) from occurring. It is estimated that more than 60 billion dollars are spent each year in the treatment of coronary heart disease and less than a million dollars yearly are spent on the prevention of this disease.

In order to prevent or slow the progress of atherosclerosis we must be aware of the *10 risk factors* which contribute to the development of this disease. One risk factor that we can't control is **heredity**; however, those people who have a strong family history of heart disease should pay particular attention to the risk factors that we can modify. The 9 risk factors which we can control ourselves or with medical treatment include: **cigarette smoking, excess alcohol consumption, excess caffeine, obesity, high blood pressure, high blood cholesterol, diabetes, stress** and **inactivity**.

One risk factor increases your risk of a heart attack by 25%. If you have two of these risk factors, it increases your likelihood of getting a heart attack by 35%. Three will increase your chances by 45% and four will increase your risk by 55-60%. If you are unfortunate enough to have five or more of these risk factors, you'd better take out a few more life insurance policies—fast!

How would you like to be able to eliminate or reduce almost all of these risk factors in one fell swoop? There is no need to worry about these risk factors if you start walking like your life depended on it. Believe me, it does! *Walking* can actually help you remove or reduce these risk factors to a minimum with a little additional help from your willpower.

How is this possible? The body that exercises doesn't want or need to *smoke* or *drink alcohol* or *caffeine*. The person who walks stays at his or her *ideal weight*. Walking lowers your *blood pressure* and your *blood cholesterol*. If you're a *diabetic* or have diabetic tendencies, walking helps to improve and regulate sugar metabolism. Walking is a sure fire method to ward off the evils of *stress* and *tension*. And, finally, walking every day completely eliminates the coronary risk factor of *inactivity*. Let's see in detail how walking alone is able to give the one-two punch to all of these coronary risk factors, without your lifting one finger, only your feet! Remember, *Walk Don't Die,* and let the coronary surgery pass you by.

1. SMOKERS SUCCUMB SWIFTLY

In a recently released study by the US Department of Agriculture, smoking causes approximately ½ million deaths every year, not 350,000 deaths as previously reported. The number of deaths that are caused either directly or indirectly from smoking are divided into:

250,000 deaths from heart disease
150,000 deaths from cancer
75,000 deaths from lung disease
5,000 deaths from fire related injuries
5,000 infant deaths from mothers' smoking
15,000 deaths from other diseases

A new study has also established a connection between smoking and a condition known as **cardiomyopathy** (failure of the heart to pump the blood). This condition affects 50,000 people every year and kills 10,000 people annually. Men under the age of 55 who smoke are 3-4 times as likely to develop this condition than non-smokers.

In a study of almost 5,000 men, reported in The New England Journal of Medicine, this condition was found among men under age 55 in 2.9 percent non-smokers, 3.6 percent medium smokers (under 1 pack per day), and 7.4 percent heavy smokers (over 1 pack per day).

This heart disorder seems to affect sedentary people more than it does those with active life-styles. **Walk, don't smoke** and leave cardiomyopathy for those stupid dopes who don't enjoy living.

Smokers by and large are a sedentary, secretive society of smoke-sucking sadists. They delight in playing Russian roulette with their lives. However, when they begin to realize that each puff brings them closer to death's door, they start to develop feelings of guilt and frustration. These feelings increase their awareness of their own mortality. So what do these masochistic, malevolent monkeys do? They become tense and anxious and smoke more cigarettes than they did before they began to think about the dangers of smoking.

Enter the walkers! By taking these sedentary smokers out into the world of oxygen, their lungs begin to extract and absorb more oxygen. Their blood supply delivers additional oxygen to their demented, deranged brain cells and carries away the excess quantities of morphine-like carbon monoxide and carbon dioxide that accumulated from the combustion of tobacco. The smoker's brain cells begin to feel the relaxing effects of the chemical endorphins from walking. These brain cells then send non-smoking messages to the smoker's will power center.

The nefarious narcotic nicotine also begins walking on its journey to the liver and kidneys for excretion from the smoker's body, into the sewers of the metropolis. Behold—the smoker begins to become a walker. He begins to lose his craving for inhaling the chemical fumes from his magic matchstick. His addiction for the stimulant nicotine starts to wane and the narcotic effect of carbon monoxide on the brain begins to lose its former control.

This smoker is not yet a walker because he can't wait to light up after a refreshing walk. But wait—he stops, lights up and lo and behold the cancerous chalklike stick has lost some of its taste and aroma. A deep inhalation leads to a fit of choking caused by his newly-found friendly lung cells, the alveoli. After their walk, these alveoli had just started sweeping out their musty, dirty closets of dust and ash when they were hit by a blast of smoke. They united one and all and used their lung billows to cough out the putrid smoke and to choke the scoundrel who tried once again to contaminate their little homes.

And so we see that the smoker has suffered his first but not his last attack from his battered body. Once given the light of day, once released from their dusty dungeon cells, these little lung cells begin to unite in a unified front to stave off the dragon's smoke. And once these little lung alveoli start to work, they never stop. They begin to load up the little carts of red blood cells with oxygen after each walk and shove them back into the bloodstream to send the oxygen message to the rest of the smoker's body's cells. Once each organ receives this fresh supply of oxygen it spews out its waste products and carbon dioxide and sends them in little boats through the bloodstream to be eliminated from the body. Their message is loud and clear—clean up your act smokers, or we won't be around to clean up after you.

And so, little by little, walk after walk the smoker and his newly discovered body work together to kick the habit. The smoker's body cells begin to transmit messages to his brain cells, which were too muddled to think before. And the message is loud and clear from each and every organ: we'll work for you as long as you don't abuse us. But if you do, we'll clog up your arteries, we'll hemorrhage your brain, we'll cancer your lungs, we'll stop your heart in its tracks. And don't think these little guys can't do it! You need them more than they need you. There are plenty of jobs out there for these friendly cells and organs. Think of how many hopeful people there are across the country just waiting to get their hands on your organs for transplants. And those people will treat your organs right!

2. ALCOHOL ATTACKS ARTERIES

Contrary to popular belief, "one drink a day" does not ward off heart disease. Although many popular magazines and newspapers have been claiming that a small amount of alcohol raises the good HDL cholesterol, they have not really done their homework well. They neglected to read the entire report of the medical articles that they couldn't quite understand. Or perhaps they were just trying to fit the facts to suit an article they wanted to write. Well, the truth of the matter is that small amounts of alcohol raise a different HDL cholesterol called subfraction-3. This particular subfraction is considered unrelated to heart disease.

The HDL cholesterol that everyone is talking about, that has a protective effect on the heart is subfraction-2. This particular subfraction-2 is not affected by any amount of alcohol. Just when the state stores and bars thought they had a good thing, the one-or-two-drinks-a-day-to-keep-the-doctor-away theory exploded in their faces. But don't worry, some smart alec reporter will make up a very convincing feature story saying that HDL cholesterol subfraction-2 is a myth and let's everyone drink up.

Now let's get down to the real facts about alcohol. Excessive consumption of alcohol is second only to cigarette smoking as a cause of preventable deaths from coronary heart disease. We won't go into the other hazards of alcohol like hepatitis, cirrhosis, liver cancer, brain damage, nerve disorders, strokes, esophageal hemorrhages, spleen enlargement, liver failure, swelling of the entire body, damage to the ovaries and testicles and so on and so forth. We'll confine ourselves to your heart or what's left of it.

Alcohol is a cardiac depressant and causes heartbeat abnormalities (arrhythmias) in more than 35% of heavy drinkers. Alcohol consumption can also cause an inflammation of the heart muscle (cardiomyopathy) often leading to heart failure. Three or more drinks daily is also associated with an increased incidence of permanent hypertension. Moderate drinking is also responsible for an elevation of the blood triglycerides, another fat which can clog up your arteries. Alcohol can also cause a chronic inflammation of the pancreas leading eventually to diabetes, which in turn can also lead to more heart disease.

There are numerous studies including those from the Chicago People Gas Co. and the Chicago Western Electric Co. which have proved beyond a reasonable doubt that excessive alcohol consumption is associated with an increased incidence of coronary artery disease. The incidence of heart attacks in these people under the age of 55 was twelve times greater than men and women the same age who did not drink.

Well now you're saying, what does all this have to do with walking? I now know that alcohol, like cigarettes, can cause heart disease, but how can walking help? Think hard. How many drinkers do you know? Have you ever seen them take a walk? Drinkers are sitters and sitters like to drink. The only exercise these folks get is bending their elbows and moving their lips. Most moderate drinkers are so-called social drinkers. They meet at bars or friends' houses to watch TV. They like to smoke, they like to sit, they like to watch, they like to talk. But they don't like to walk. Show me a walker and I'll show you a non-drinker.

Walkers get their highs (endorphins) and kicks (oxygen) from walking. They don't need to drink to relax. Walking at the end of a stressful day relaxes the body more than any amount of alcohol can and without the side effects. Drinkers get an initial stimulation from alcohol followed rapidly by depression and lethargy. They can't even remember if they were relaxed at all. The initial effects are short-lived but the after-effects linger on and on.

If you can get a drinker to start walking every day,

I'll guarantee that you'll get him to stop drinking. Walking is the only oxygen and tonic drink that anyone needs to feel relaxed, reduce stress and stay healthy. Walking every day reduces the urge to drink, because of the increased oxygen supply to all of the body's cells. Also the mood calming effect of the increased brain chemicals (endorphins), relaxes the drinker without the use of alcohol. Next time you're meeting a friend, whether it's business or social, instead of saying how about a drink, say let's take a walk and talk. And I'll bet you didn't know that walkers are the best lovers and drinkers are about the worst because of their low hormone levels. Also remember, don't drink and drive; better yet, don't drink—just walk!

3. CAFFEINE CHOKES CORONARIES, CAUSES CANCER AND CANCELS CALCIUM

Caffeine has been shown to definitely elevate blood pressure, especially in those people who are predisposed to developing hypertension. Excessive caffeine can also cause abnormal heart rhythms (arrhythmias), ranging from simple palpitations to life-threatening irregular heartbeats. More recent studies have now linked excessive coffee consumption with the development of *coronary heart disease.*

If you drink more than 2½ cups of coffee a day, you will elevate your total serum cholesterol and the bad LDL cholesterol in your bloodstream. Drinking coffee also elevates two other harmful fats in your blood: the triglycerides and one type of fat called the apolipoprotein B fraction, both of which can also clog up your arteries. Too much coffee also gets rid of your good HDL cholesterol which helps to protect you from heart disease.

It's beginning to sound like there's nothing around anymore that's good for you. The rule of thumb seems to be that if it looks good and smells good and tastes good, you probably can't have it. Well, in this case, at least, there is an alternative. Even though tea has caffeine in it, although not as much as coffee, it does not seem to cause as many abnormalities in the blood fats. Nor does tea seem to increase blood pressure or cause coronary artery disease. At this point in time, no one seems to know the reasons, but there appear to be some unknown chemicals or agents in coffee that are not present in tea. Even decaffeinated coffee may cause some of these blood fat abnormalities whereas decaffeinated tea does not.

The fact remains that one cup of coffee a day will probably not do you any harm. You should always take a cup of decaffeinated coffee as your second cup. Or better yet, just switch to decaffeinated tea and see your blood pressure and blood fats return to normal levels.

Other effects of excessive caffeine use are: insomnia, nervousness, anxiety, vomiting, rapid heartbeat, shortness of breath, excessive urination and perspiration, and on rare occasions hallucinations, mental confusion and convulsions. Recent studies have also suggested a possible link between excessive caffeine use in coffee drinkers to *cancers of the bladder, pancreas* and *breast;* and to *fibrocystic breast disease.*

The best alternative to coffee and even tea is walking. Instead of sitting idly sipping caffeine at the end of your meal, you should be outside drinking in the fresh air as you walk off at least part of your meal's calories. Next time instead of a coffee break, take a walk break away from stress and tension. We get enough stimulation from our lives and jobs each day. Caffeine is the last thing in the world that we need for rest and relaxation. It's much better to walk and talk than sit and sip. If you want to stay calm and serene, stay away from caffeine (**TABLE V**).

TABLE V
APPROXIMATE CAFFEINE CONTENT IN
COMMON DRINKS AND DRUG PREPARATIONS

Regular coffee (cup)	75-100 mg
Instant coffee (cup)	60-100 mg
Decaffeinated coffee (cup)	2-10 mg
Tea (cup)	30-60 mg
Decaffeinated tea (cup)	1-8 mg
Cola drinks (12 oz.)	25-60 mg
Per tablet or dose	
APC	32 mg
Cafergot	100 mg
Fiorinal	40 mg
Anacin	32 mg
Bromo-Seltzer	32 mg
Excedrin	60 mg
Dristan	30 mg
Vivarin	200 mg
No-Doz	100 mg

Here is the final nail in caffeine's coffin: A new study shows that caffeine also robs the body of calcium. Caffeine promotes calcium loss by interfering with the kidney's ability to re-absorb calcium. Coffee drinkers who consume regular coffee instead of decaffeinated coffee lose 50% more calcium and are subject to weakened bones and hypertension.

4. DIABETES:
DANGEROUS DISEASE

Numerous studies have documented the fact that men and women with diabetes have a higher incidence of coronary heart disease than non-diabetic people. The Framingham study in particular noted a significant increase in the incidence of heart disease in both diabetic men and women.

Diabetes appears to increase the rate of atherosclerosis in the arteries. This occurs because diabetic people have higher bad LDL-cholesterol and lower good HDL-cholesterol in their blood. They are usually overweight and have a tendency to develop hypertension more often. They also have high levels of serum triglycerides (sugar fats) in their blood which is related to their elevated blood sugar. Diabetics are at greater risk for developing complications following heart attacks, like irregular heartbeats and heart failure.

There are essentially two types of diabetes. Type I is called *insulin-dependent* or *juvenile diabetes*. It usually occurs in young people but can also occur in middle age. In this type of diabetes the pancreas lacks the ability to make sufficient amounts of insulin and the person must take daily injections of insulin to control the blood sugar. This type of diabetes is the most difficult type to control and is often referred to as brittle diabetes.

Type II diabetes is known as *noninsulin-dependent* or *maturity-onset diabetes*. This type generally occurs in later life (40 years or older) and usually in overweight individuals. In this type of diabetes the pancreas can produce insulin but in some cases more than normal amounts are produced. The problem here is that many of the cells throughout the body lack what are called *receptor sites,* so they are unable to receive the available insulin. These cells then are unable to perform their regular functions because they can't metabolize or process sugar properly without insulin. Since these cells can't produce energy without sugar, they begin to malfunction. This type of diabetes usually responds favorably to diet, weight loss and sometimes oral medication.

Moderate exercises like walking are particularly important in managing diabetes. When you walk, your blood sugar (glucose) level drops and carbohydrates are used more effectively. This results in normal fat and protein metabolism. The main point in diabetes control is to keep the blood glucose as near the normal range as possible. Food increases your blood sugar level and exercise and insulin decrease the blood sugar. Therefore, the diabetic must continually balance diet, insulin and exercise to keep his blood sugar normal.

Walking improves the utilization of glucose by the body and increases the body's cells' sensitivity to insulin. Walking may actually allow the diabetic to reduce his dosage of insulin or oral medication. In the non-insulin-dependent diabetic who is usually overweight, walking burns calories and leads to weight loss. This results in an increase in muscle mass and a decrease in body fat, which produces an improvement in glucose metabolism. By improving the control of diabetes, walking indirectly reduces the risk of cardiovascular disease.

Strenuous exercise, on the other hand, can have a detrimental effect on the diabetic. Vigorous prolonged exercise may actually drop the blood sugar too rapidly causing sudden hypoglycemia with shock-like symptoms. Also, some diabetic complications which affect the eye, kidney and nerves may be worsened by strenuous exercise. And, finally, diabetics may have coronary artery disease with no symptoms at all. Strenuous exercise in these people could lead to irregular heartbeats or heart attacks.

No form of exercise, even walking, will completely cure diabetes. However, combined with good medical care, proper diet and medication, walking can be an important adjunct in controlling diabetes and its complications. With proper diabetic control, walking can help to reduce this risk factor as a cause of coronary heart disease.

It is also a good idea, even for those people without diabetes, to stay away from refined sugar (cake, candy, pie, ice-cream, soda and most desserts). There appears to be a higher incidence of heart disease, diabetes and obesity in people who consume large quantities of refined sugars. This is especially important if you have a family history of diabetes.

5. CHOLESTEROL CLOGS CORONARIES

Many studies have demonstrated a significant correlation between dietary cholesterol and coronary heart disease. A recent Japanese study demonstrated that Japanese men had lower blood cholesterol and lower coronary heart disease than Japanese-American men living in San Francisco. This was due entirely to the high fat diet consumed by the Japanese-American men.

An international study using 18 different population groups living in eleven countries showed a direct correlation between fat and cholesterol intake and coronary heart disease. The lower the blood cholesterol, the lower the incidence of heart disease.

In a national cooperative pooling project research group, middle aged men were studied in several different groups (Albany Gas Co., Chicago Gas & Electric companies, Framingham and Tecumeseh studies). All of these various studies pooled together showed a significant relationship between serum cholesterol and the ten-year risk of developing heart disease. In each study the conclusion was the same: the lower your blood cholesterol, the lower your incidence of developing heart disease.

The relationship between high cholesterol in your blood and coronary heart disease has been demonstrated by so many studies that the proof is now irrefutable. If your serum cholesterol is below 200 mg and stays there, you are virtually immune to coronary artery disease.

The role of elevated serum triglycerides in causing coronary heart disease in some studies is controversial; however, most studies have definitely found some relationship. Many other diseases are associated with high serum triglycerides. They include diabetes, obesity, thyroid disorders and certain kidney diseases.

Since elevated triglycerides often accompany elevated LDL-cholesterol levels, they are indirectly related to the development of early coronary artery disease.

Since cholesterol will not dissolve in your bloodstream, it must attach itself to a protein. These proteins act as a ship transporting its passenger (cholesterol) through your bloodstream. And now we will take a little journey across the ocean as we go "down to the sea in ships." First we'll travel on the sinister pirate ship called the LDL and then we'll take a little cruise across the sea of blood in the good ship Lolly-Pop.

The **BAD-CHOLESTEROL, PIRATE-SHIP** (**LDL**-low density lipo-protein combination) deposits cholesterol in your arteries when you eat too much cholesterol or saturated fat. If you limit the amount of **saturated fat** and **cholesterol-rich foods** that you eat, the bad pirate-ship will have less cholesterol to carry around and it won't be able to block up your arteries with its cargo of fat. You can sink the bad-cholesterol, pirate-ship before it torpedoes your heart. If you stuff your face with fatty foods, you'll surely walk the pirate's gangplank to an early watery grave.

New medical evidence has found that there's another way to sink this pirate ship. A daily walk around the ship's deck will prevent these pirate plunderers from dumping cholesterol into arteries. Regular walkers have less LDL cholesterol and less triglycerides than those passengers who just sit on the deck sunning themselves.

The **GOOD-CHOLESTEROL-SHIP, LOLLY-POP** (**HDL**-high density lipo-protein combination) flies a different flag. It rams the pirate ship, by collecting the excess amounts of cholesterol in the blood and taking it to the liver where it is eliminated from the body in little barrels of bile juices. Recent medical studies indicate that the sailors on this good-ship, lolly-pop (**HDL**) may also be able to remove the cholesterol that has already formed in your arteries and dump it out at sea.

How do we get aboard this good-ship, lolly-pop (**HDL CHOLESTEROL**)? Heredity plays an important part in the production of **HDL** cholesterol. Some of us have more HDL cholesterol than others because of a good set of genes. Diet unfortunately has almost no effect in **HDL** production—so a low fat, low cholesterol diet won't budge your HDL cholesterol; however, it will certainly lower the bad LDL cholesterol.

There is however, one thing that you can do to increase the production of **HDL**. You guessed it! Our old tried and true friend—**WALKING**—will raise your **HDL** levels. If you walk ½ hour daily or 1 hour every other day, you will keep your **HDL** permanently elevated. High intensity exercises like jogging for brief periods of time raise the **HDL** level temporarily and then it falls after the exercise is completed.

A nice long walk every day is the only way to keep the good-cholesterol-ship, lolly-pop afloat. By carrying its cargo of fat out of your body, your heart will live to sail another day.

THE OTHER 5 RISK FACTORS THAT YOU CAN ALSO WALK OFF

6. OBESITY: Previously covered in Chapter 7—**"IT'S NO FUN TO BE FAT."**

7. INACTIVITY: Previously covered in Chapter 10— **"SEDENTARY SITTERS SUCCUMB SOONER."**

8. HYPERTENSION: Next Chapter 14— **"STRESS-STEP: WALKING AROUND KEEPS BLOOD PRESSURE DOWN."**

9. STRESS: Next Chapter 14—
"STRESS-STEP:
WALKING AROUND
KEEPS BLOOD
PRESSURE DOWN."

10. HEREDITY: If you happen to be unlucky
enough to have been slipped
a bad heart disease gene by
one of your parents, don't
worry. If you walk regularly,
you'll be able to walk off all
of the other 9 coronary risk
factors. And as far as a bad
gene or two goes, it's better
to walk around with a couple
of defective genes than not
to be able to walk around at
all.

*   *   *   *   *   *   *

Walk, Don't Die **and you'll let the risk factors of
heart disease pass you by.**

CHAPTER 14

STRESS-STEP: WALKING AROUND KEEPS BLOOD PRESSURE DOWN

KEEP YOUR FEET ON THE GROUND & YOUR BLOOD PRESSURE DOWN

According to the American Heart Association more than one out of every four people in the United States has high blood pressure. Among people age 65 years and older, approximately two out of three people suffer from hypertension. There are approximately 57.7 million Americans who have high blood pressure according to the Heart Association Council for High Blood Pressure Research. Many of these people are at considerable risk for developing strokes, heart attacks, heart failure and kidney disease, unless they receive medical treatment. Unfortunately most people with high blood pressure have no symptoms and may have hypertension for many years before it is diagnosed. Remember, always get your blood pressure checked regularly.

Many cases of mild hypertension can be controlled without the use of medication. These methods include weight reduction, salt restriction, cessation of smoking, alcohol restriction, decreasing saturated fats and cholesterol in the diet, stress reduction and exercise. It should be pointed out that the majority of studies on the benefits of exercise for lowering blood pressure, have used walking as the best moderate intensity exercise for this purpose. Jogging and other strenuous exercises can actually raise blood pressure during the actual exercise.

An Oslo research study of approximately 18,000 men aged 40-49 years recorded lower blood pressures in those men who engaged in regular leisure activity, particularly walking and gardening. Interestingly, no blood pressure differences were noted among different intensities of physical exercise which again emphasizes the point that faster is not necessarily better.

Two major studies reported in a recent issue of the Journal of the American Medical Association proved without a doubt that regular exercise, particularly walking, can decrease the risk of developing heart disease and high blood pressure by more than 50 percent.

The first report from the Research Institute in Dallas studied over 6,000 men and women who had no previous history of high blood pressure. Over a period of 4 years, people who did not exercise regularly ran a 52 percent higher risk of developing hypertension. The second study from Harvard University followed 17,000 men over a period of 16 years (from 1962 to 1978). Those men who exercised regularly experienced only one-half the death rate from heart disease and hypertension. This study showed lower blood pressures in those alumni that regularly participated in vigorous sports as well as in those alumni who just walked regularly. The fact still remains that you get the same cardiovascular benefits, in this case lower blood pressure, from walking as you do from more strenuous sports without the hazards.

In a related study reported in the journal Athero-sclerosis (Dec., 1983), high risk men ages 43 to 60 were tested with a low-fat diet only, and were compared to a similar group which combined the low-fat diet with a walking program. The group that also walked had a significant reduction in weight, cholesterol, triglycer-ides, total body fat and blood pressure compared with only moderate reductions in the group that only diet-ed.

In no fewer than seven other separate studies in hypertensive men and women, a walking program pro-duced lowered blood pressure in over 80% of these patients. The periods of exercise training varied in these different studies from three months to three years. It was interesting to note also, that if any pa-tient dropped out of the program, his/her blood pres-sure gradually went up to its former hypertensive level after six-eight weeks. This confirmed the theory that in order for exercise to be beneficial, particularly for high blood pressure, it must be carried on for a life-time. And what better exercise than walking can be done for the rest of your life?

The medical evidence is overwhelming that regu-lar exercise, particularly walking, lowers the blood pressure in people with hypertension. There is also increasing evidence that a regular program of walking can help to prevent hypertension from developing in those individuals who have a hereditary predisposition or tendency to develop high blood pressure. There have also been many recent studies on children, showing that the inactive child is more likely to become the obese hypertensive adult than the child who exercises regularly.

There are several physiological mechanisms re-sponsible for the blood pressure lowering effect of exer-cise. They include improved cardiac output of blood, decreased peripheral vascular resistance to the flow of blood, slower pulse rate, dilation of small arteries, thinning of the blood and a reduced release of catecholamines and angiotensin (the hormones that cause high blood pressure). The fact remains, however, that no matter what the physiological reasons are, walking lowers your blood pressure. All you have to remember is that if you **keep your feet on the ground, you'll keep your blood pressure down!**

HOW TO "SHAKE" THE SALT HABIT

Throwing away the salt shaker is almost as difficult as giving up cigarettes for most of us. Salt is hazardous to the health of the 40-50 million Americans who are at risk for developing *hypertension*. And what makes it even worse is that no one really knows who's at risk, until he or she actually develops hypertension, and in many cases that's too late.

The hesitancy about giving up salt is the fear that food will never taste the same again. Take heart, it takes approximately 10-12 weeks for the taste buds to adjust to no salt and then surprisingly—**food actually tastes better**. Here are a few tips on how to shake the salt habit:

1. Drink water with your meals to evenly disperse the flavor of foods.
2. Use herbs, vinegar, spices, lemon juice and wine to accent flavor.
3. Pepper, garlic and cloves can be substituted for salt.
4. Salt substitutes can be used, with your doctor's permission.
5. Remember, you get 3-5 times the amount of salt your body needs every day from the foods you eat, without adding one grain of salt to your food.

6. Stay away from salted pretzels, potato and corn chips and most processed packaged snack food.
7. Substitute fresh fruits and vegetables for between meal snacks.
8. Switch to foods with a high potassium content since they seem to help lower blood pressure. Oranges, grapefruit, bananas, tomatoes, potatoes, cabbage, squash, broccoli, turkey and chicken are all high potassium foods.

STRESS SLAUGHTERS SWIFTLY

Emotional stress can precipitate heart attacks in patients with a history of coronary artery disease. Type A behavior (high-strung, aggressive personalities) has also been associated with an increased incidence of coronary heart disease, completely independent of other coronary risk factors (The Western Collaborative Group Study: Am. J. Cardiology, Vol. 37, 1976). And patients who already had coronary heart disease with Type A behavior were shown to have more severe artery involvement than did patients with heart disease who had Type B behavior (non-aggressive, more relaxed type personalities).

In another related study (The Recurrent Coronary Prevention Project: Am. Heart J., Vol. 108, 1984) counseling of Type A heart patients resulted in a reduction of Type A behavior in 44% of those counseled. These patients whose high strung emotional behavior was modified, had 20% less recurrent heart attacks than the Type A heart patients who did not receive counseling.

It is well documented that emotional stress can not only contribute to the development of heart disease but that it can also aggravate existing coronary artery disease. Stress can aggravate angina pectoris (heart pain from poor circulation in the coronary arteries) in patients who have coronary artery disease. When stressed, these people may develop severe chest pain that can usually be relieved by putting a nitroglycerine tablet under their tongues.

Stress can also precipitate heart attacks (myocardial infarctions), heartbeat irregularities (arrhythmias) and sudden cardiac arrest, in patients with pre-existing coronary artery disease. A recent study reported in The New England Journal of Medicine (Vol. 311, 1984) showed an increased risk of cardiac deaths among men with high levels of stress, who had previously survived a heart attack. And emotional stress combined with excess salt in the diet may actually cause some people to develop a permanent form of high blood pressure (Figs. 4 & 5).

All of these studies prove that emotional stress can cause coronary heart disease as well as aggravate it in patients who already have heart disease. And all of these studies also show that by reducing stress, coronary heart disease and hypertension can often be prevented in normal patients and controlled in patients who already have heart or blood pressure problems. Type A behavior can be modified with stress management techniques. These techniques include personal counseling, avoiding stressful situations, and our true, blue, loyal friend—*walking*. Walking has been proven over and over again to significantly reduce stress and tension, alleviate anger and hostility, decrease fatigue and malaise, and control anxiety and depression. Walk away from stress today and your heart will be O.K.

TYPE A's SPIN THEIR WHEELS ALL DAY

Type A personalities, because of their competitive nature, do not do well in jobs that require team effort. Recent studies at Michigan State University Medical

School revealed that Type A's had significantly higher heart rates and blood pressures than Type B personality types during office hours. EKG readings also showed that Type A hearts even get less oxygen when their blood pressures and heart rates rise. The Type A's spend most of their time competing with their co-workers rather than doing their jobs. This type of person does poorly in most job profiles that require team effort and team spirit.

Many runners who by nature are competitive, also have Type A aggressive personalities. This fact may account for the recent upsurge in sudden deaths in apparently healthy runners. According to a recent study reported in American Health, **competitive thoughts** during strenuous exercise raise the levels of the stress hormones (*epinephrine* and *norepinephrine*) in the bloodstream, which puts a strain on the heart. These hormones can damage the heart and arteries by causing irregular heartbeats, electrolyte abnormalities and blood clotting. These factors may lead to an increased risk of a sudden heart attack when combined with the strenuous exertion of running.

Walkers, on the other hand, are more even-tempered than runners and rarely are competitive by nature. Walking is a more relaxed type of activity and walkers take a more casual approach to exercise. Competitive thinking with its resultant damaging stress hormones is rarely a problem for the walker as compared to the runner who must push faster and harder than the next guy. Don't bother to get in their way, just let the Type A's spin their wheels all day.

IT'S AS EASY AS A-B-C

Type A personality women under stress are at higher risk for heart attacks than Type B personality women. Recent research has shown that these competitive, aggressive women have the same high risk of

FIGURE 4
Stress and Salt in Hypertension

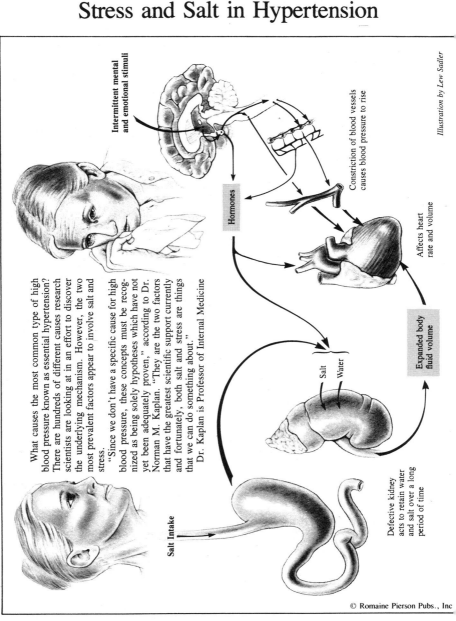

Illustration by Lew Sadler

Intermittent mental and emotional stimuli

Constriction of blood vessels causes blood pressure to rise

Hormones

Affects heart rate and volume

What causes the most common type of high blood pressure known as essential hypertension? There are hundreds of different causes research scientists are looking at in an effort to discover the underlying mechanism. However, the two most prevalent factors appear to involve salt and stress.

"Since we don't have a specific cause for high blood pressure, these concepts must be recognized as being solely hypotheses which have not yet been adequately proven," according to Dr. Norman M. Kaplan. "They are the two factors that have the greatest scientific support currently and fortunately, both salt and stress are things that we can do something about."

Dr. Kaplan is Professor of Internal Medicine

Expanded body fluid volume

Salt

Water

Salt Intake

Defective kidney acts to retain water and salt over a long period of time

© Romaine Pierson Pubs., Inc

"Courtesy of Medical Times"

FIGURE 5

and Director of the Hypertension Service, the U of Texas Southwestern Medical School.

"It is true in animals and it is probably true in people, too, that regardless of what you do to make blood pressure go up, permanent hypertension will develop only in those with an inherited predisposition to the disease," says Dr. Kaplan. We know from studies that the likelihood of a person developing hypertension is about twice as high if either of the parents were hypertensive. There is little question that we are dealing at least in part with a hereditary problem, compounded by factors from the environment. The two that have the most scientific support currently are salt and stress, he believes.

Salt presumably acts by being retained with water by the kidneys over a long period of time. This expands the total fluid volume in the body, increasing the output from the heart and essentially overfilling the circulation that sets off the hypertension process.

"However, we must also assume that there is something defective in the kidney because if the kidneys were perfectly normal, they would simply get rid of any extra salt, says Dr. Kaplan.

The second factor is stress and both salt and stress could be related, according to Dr. Kaplan.

Evidence points to hypertension starting because of repeated, intermittent stress which sets off the sympathetic nervous system in susceptible people. The sympathetic nerves then cause the blood vessels to constrict and while the stress is going on, the blood pressure rises.

"Everyone has seen this happen. Just going into a doctor's office can cause some patient's first blood pressure reading to be higher. When the patient relaxes, the blood pressure reading tends to go down some. Over a prolonged period of time, there are actual structural changes that go on in the blood vessels of the person under stress. The stress increases the release of hormones by the sympathetic nervous system which causes changes within the kidney. The changes that go on in the kidney cause extra fluid to be retained due to the increase in sympathetic nervous system activity.

"The idea is that at first this phenomenon is an intermittent process and only causes the blood pressure to go up when the person is under stress. But after a while, even when the person is relaxed, certain changes that cause the blood pressure to stay up have been produced which could then be the beginning of what we know as persistent or permanent high blood pressure."

But even more likely to help and more easily to

be accomplished is a decrease in dietary sodium intake. There is no possible harm in reducing our daily salt intake by a half and there is a great potential value in reducing the incidence of hypertension. Simply by not using salt in cooking, nor at the table, and avoiding highly salted foods, we may be postponing or preventing the major risk for premature heart attacks and strokes.

Sodium Content of Some Processed Foods

	Amount	Sodium (mgs)
Tomato catsup (Heinz)	1 tbsp.	182
Frankfurter, beef (Oscar Mayer)	1	425
Bologna (Oscar Mayer)	2 slices	450
Tomato Juice (Del Monte)	1 cup	640
Cinnamon Rolls (Pillsbury)	1	630
Chicken noodle soup (Campbells)	10 oz.	1050
Frozen turkey dinner (Swanson)	1	1735
Pickle, dill	1 large	1928

Fruits and Vegetables That Are Low in Calories, Low in Sodium, High in Potassium

(Less than 100 calories and 50 mg sodium, more than 200 mg of potassium per serving)

Artichoke	Orange
Banana	Orange juice
Broccoli	Peach
Brussels sprouts	Potato
Cantaloupe	Strawberries
Carrots	Tomato
Honeydew melon	Watermelon

Similar Foods With Low and High Sodium Content

Low	High
Shredded Wheat 1 mg/oz	Corn Flakes, 305 mg/oz
Green Beans, fresh, 5 mg/cup	Green Beans, canned 925 mg/cup
Orange Juice, 2 mg/cup	Tomato Juice, 640 mg/cup
Turkey, roasted, 70 mg/3 oz	Turkey dinner, frozen 1735 mg
Ground Beef, 57 mg/3 oz	Frankfurter, beef, 425 mg

From a Symposium on Hypertension sponsored by the University of Arizona College of Medicine and Ciba Pharmaceutical Company.

© Romaine Pierson Pubs., Inc.

"Courtesy of Medical Times"

heart attacks as Type A men. These women also have a higher incidence of diabetes, hypertension, strokes and peptic ulcer disease.

In a study of over 1,200 women, the Type A women when compared to Type B women were found to have the following characteristics:
1. Drink more than 3-4 cups of coffee daily.
2. Smoke 1-2 packs cigarettes daily.
3. Overweight by 8-15 pounds.
4. Exhibit chronic anger and resentment.
5. No regular form of exercise.

These women, whether in the work force or at home, were found to be more aggressive and competitive, more independent, less able to relax and have more unhappy marriages than Type B's.

I can almost guarantee that walking can change any woman into a Type B or least an A-minus personality. Walking can rid the body of stress and tension, decrease the need to smoke, control the weight and give a feeling of peace and contentment. Anger, resentment, frustration and stress can't exist in a peaceful environment. She'll still be an A-minus or B-plus personality, never a Type C (calm). Walking will still give her the necessary independent, competitive edge needed in business or at home, but without the risks of heart attacks, hypertension, strokes and ulcers.

WALK, DON'T CRY!

Walking can combat the health hazards of stress and tension. Walking is as good for mental fitness as it is for physical fitness. Being physically fit goes hand-in-hand with mental fitness. The trick about dealing with stress is not to deal with it. Walk away from stress, I mean literally take a walk away from any stressful situation. Stress comes in many forms—frustration, boredom, too much responsibility, not enough time to do what you want to do, family problems, job-related stresses and pressure from all sorts of people. These are all part of the game of stress. Beat stress at its own game, and you'll live to walk away sane.

Researchers from New York's Memorial Sloan-Kettering Cancer Institute and other major universities have discovered that stress and depression can even make people more susceptible to developing cancer. The theory behind this startling piece of evidence is that cancer cells probably are in our bodies all the time. When we are subject to stress and suppress our emotions, our body's immune system becomes inactive and we are unable to fight off diseases including cancer cells.

Women seem to be at a higher risk than men for developing cancer because of personality and psychological factors. Women repress their feelings of anger more than men do and frequently suffer from depression when under emotional stress. These suppressed emotions seem to cause a malfunction in the immune system causing cancer cells to become active.

The body's delicate chemical balance is maintained at an even keel by *walking off stress*. Walking clears the mind, vents emotional anger and dissipates depression and helps the body's natural defense system (immune system) to fight off disease and, in this particular case, cancer. Walk as if your life depended on it. It probably does! **Walk, Don't Cry**, don't let stress make you die.

STRESS-STEP STOPS STROKES

Strokes are the third leading cause of deaths in the United States each year. The most frequent contributing factor is high blood pressure. Approximately 65% of all strokes occur in people who never knew they had high blood pressure or in people who had hypertension but did not take their medication regularly.

High blood pressure speeds up the process of

atherosclerosis ("hardening of the arteries"). Untreated hypertension damages the lining walls of the arteries and allows fatty deposits to collect in the arteries. This in turn sets the stage for blood clots to form in the blood vessels of the brain, which can cause a stroke. High blood pressure also can weaken the walls of the blood vessels so that a balloon or aneurysm forms. The combination of high blood pressure and extreme physical exertion (example: jogging, weight-lifting, etc.) may cause this aneurysm to rupture, which results in a hemorrhage into the brain producing another form of stroke.

Fortunately, stroke-related deaths have declined by almost 45% in the United States in the past 10 years. This is due primarily to the widespread, successful treatment of high blood pressure. People are beginning to realize that they have to continue taking their high blood pressure medicine indefinitely, in order to prevent strokes from occurring.

Stopping smoking also is important in preventing strokes from occurring. The carbon monoxide from smoking damages the blood vessel walls, and speeds up the process of atherosclerosis. The early treatment of diabetes and obesity also helps to slow down this process of hardening of the arteries, which leads to hypertension and stroke. And we have already seen how the avoidance of salt and stress helps to lower blood pressure and in turn reduces your risk of stroke.

According to most medical authorities, a moderate program of regular exercise is extremely important in controlling high blood pressure and in preventing strokes. You heard it—moderate exercise! Walking is the exercise most often prescribed by physicians to control hypertension. Walking lowers the blood pressure and can help to prevent strokes. The following 12 steps show you in detail how the *Stress-Step* actually lowers your blood pressure.

THE STRESS-STEP LOWERS YOUR BLOOD PRESSURE BY:

1. Improving the efficiency of the lungs to take up oxygen from the atmosphere.
2. Improving the cardiac output (total volume of blood pumped out by the heart each minute), so that the heart can work more efficiently at a slower rate.
3. Increasing the amount of oxygen delivered to all the cells and tissues in the body.
4. Improving the return of blood to the heart from the leg and abdominal veins by utilizing the leg's muscle pumping action.
5. Dilating (opening) the blood vessels and making them more elastic and flexible, giving less resistance to the flow of blood.
6. Decreasing the formation of chemicals in the blood known as catecholamines and angiotensin—(high blood levels of these chemicals may cause high blood pressure).
7. Increasing relaxation hormones in the brain—Beta-endorphins and decreasing the formation of the stress hormones (epinephrine and norepinephrine).
8. Increasing the oxygen supply to the brain and decreasing its carbon dioxide level.
9. Increasing the total volume of blood including red blood cells, thus allowing a greater supply of oxygen to be carried in the bloodstream.
10. Decreasing the chance of clot formation by preventing the blood platelets from sticking together.
11. Decreasing the rate of sodium (salt) reabsorption in the kidneys, preventing salt from being put back into the bloodstream.
12. Literally walking away from stress—don't let stress make you sigh—*Walk, Don't Die.*

"I TOLD MY DOCTOR THAT GOLF EVERY WEDNESDAY WASN'T ENOUGH EXERCISE!"

CHAPTER 15

LIFESTEP: STEPS TO PREVENT YOUR DEATH

OLD WALKERS NEVER DIE

A recent survey of over 1,200 men and women over the age of 80 showed that all of these people were physically active. And over 90 percent of them stated that walking was their only exercise. The more active you are the less likely you are to be plagued with the degenerative diseases of aging. It is never too late to begin a walking program, even after years of inactivity. The body responds to exercise at any time and at any age.

The human body is one of the few machines that breaks down when it's not used. A physically active person is one who is both mentally and physically alert. A walking program will actually slow down the aging process and add years to your life. Walking stimulates a healthy circulation, aids in cardiovascular fitness, improves muscle tone and bone strength, and improves the oxygen uptake and distribution to all the tissues and cells of the body. People who lead inactive lives often seem to develop early deterioration in their mental and physical faculties. Inactivity often leads to depression, frustration, general weakness and lethargy. Walking is the best way to release pent-up energy and emotion and can lead to a more physically active life.

Walking is the magic elixir of youth for both the body and the mind. As you walk your blood is pumped out by your heart, into your arteries and then into the smaller blood vessels called the arterioles and then into the tiny capillaries. It is here that the blood gives up its valuable supply of oxygen and nutrients to all of our body's cells and tissues. If the cells are constantly saturated with oxygen they will age at a much slower rate than cells that do not get enough oxygen (example: people who sit all day). Increased oxygenation is actually what slows the aging process. If you walk every day, I guarantee that you'll live longer than any of your sedentary friends. Walking is the only exercise that will last you a lifetime, and *walking will make that lifetime last!*

LIVE 100 YEARS WITHOUT FEAR

The actual aging process results from a number of biochemical and physiological reactions that occur at the cellular level. These changes which occur over a number of years result in a degeneration or aging of the cells and tissues in our body. The only way to slow down this aging process is to keep all of the cells constantly saturated with oxygen and nutrients supplied by the blood. And the only way to keep the blood rich in oxygen and nutrients is to eat a balanced diet and to walk every day. Let's see how the various organs and systems in our bodies age, and how walking can slow down this aging process.

1. Cardiovascular System:

Your heart's ability to pump blood slowly decreases approximately 4-5% every 8-10 years after the age of 35. This means that your heart is unable to pump as much blood throughout the body with each heartbeat as you get older. As you age your blood vessels lose some of their elasticity because of the accumulation of fat and calcium in the artery walls. This can impair the general circulation because the arteries cannot expand properly to accomodate the blood pumped into them by the heart. This increased resistance to the flow of blood accounts for the gradual increase in your blood pressure by approximately 5-6% every 8-10 years after the age of 35.

Walking can actually slow down the aging process of the cardiovascular system. Walking strengthens the heart muscle and improves the cardiac output (volume of blood pumped out by the heart). It also regulates the pumping action of the heart at a slower, more efficient heart rate. Regular walking also prevents the gradual rise in blood pressure by keeping the blood vessels more flexible and by decreasing the amount of fatty deposits that accumulate in your arteries. These factors are what prevent walkers from getting heart attacks, high blood pressure and strokes.

2. Respiratory System:

The aging lung shows a gradual decrease in its elastic recoil or resiliency after the age of 30. As we age there is also a moderate decrease in the ability of the chest wall muscles and the diaphragm to assist in breathing. What this means is that the lung loses some of its ability to expand and then contract with each breath that we take in and blow out. These lung changes found in the aging lung are somewhat similar to those findings found in people who smoke and have started to develop early emphysema. The main difference, however, is that these lung changes found in the aging lung are minimal compared to the smoker's lung, and they are completely reversible with exercise, whereas the changes in the emphysematous lung are permanent.

Regular walking improves the resiliency of the lung tissue and subsequently makes the lungs more efficient in taking oxygen in from the air, and blowing out carbon dioxide from the lung. Walking also aids in opening more usable lung surface (alveoli) for the exchange of oxygen and carbon dioxide. And finally, regular exercise conditions the chest wall and diaphragm muscles so that they work more efficiently in breathing and respiration. Walking can also be helpful in improving the breathing capacity in people with asthma, emphysema and other chronic lung disorders. These patients however, should be monitored carefully by their physicians.

3. **Musculo-Skeletal System:**

As you age, you lose actual muscle mass at a rate of approximately 3-5% every 10 years. Aging also causes an actual decrease in bone density, which is due to the loss of the calcium mineral content of the bone. This occurs at a rate of 4-6% every decade. This calcium loss eventually thins and weakens the bone (osteoporosis). Both the loss of muscle mass and bone density result in a gradual decrease of strength and endurance. Muscles also gradually lose their resiliency and elasticity over the years. This results in a slowing of the reaction time, making motor functions like driving dangerous.

Walking can strengthen the individual muscle fibers and help to prevent the actual loss of muscle tissue. The exercised muscles exert a tension or muscular pull on the bones to which they are attached. This tension helps to preserve bone structure, bone strength and muscle elasticity. The decrease in bone density caused by the loss of calcium from the bones can actually be reversed by a walking program combined with a high calcium diet. Walking can therefore help to prevent osteoporosis from occurring. It can also help to prevent or control the symptoms of certain forms of degenerative musculo-skeletal disorders (example: osteoarthritis).

4. Longevity System:

There is no doubt about it. If you are inactive you will age faster. A sedentary life-style is a major factor in the acceleration of all of these physiological changes which result in the aging process. A lifetime walking program may actually be the only defense that we have against the degenerative diseases of aging. Many medical studies have shown that the maximum oxygen consumption declines with age at a rate of 1% per year after the age of 25. These studies have also shown that regular exercise slows down this decline.

Walking increases the body's maximum oxygen consumption by improving the efficiency of the cardio-vascular, respiratory and musculo-skeletal systems. This oxygen is the vital ingredient necessary for the production of energy and the prevention of aging at the cell's molecular level. In effect, walking provides us with an easy, foolproof method to slow or retard the aging process. These statistics don't lie—*Walk, Don't Die!*

A regular lifetime walking program results in an improved heart and lung capacity with more efficient function; improved oxygen uptake by the heart muscle and tissues of the body; improved utilization of blood sugar for energy; and an increase in lean body mass. Regular exercise not only benefits the lung and circulatory systems but helps to maintain body weight, preserves bone structure and muscle tone, and relieves stress and tension. A regular walking program will also combat anxiety and depression that so often affects the elderly and will help them to develop a positive self-image. We may retire from our jobs in life, but we cannot retire from our life—*walking is the key to a long, healthful and happy life.*

CIRCULATING, PERCOLATING, LIFE-SUSTAINING BLOOD

Your heart acts as a pump supplying the force necessary to propel your blood through the vast network of blood vessels. The blood travels first through the *arteries* which have both elastic and muscular walls allowing them to stretch and then recoil, thus helping to propel the blood along their course. The blood next passes through the smaller arteries known as *arterioles* which actually regulate the blood pressure. They accomplish this by narrowing their passages (lumens) in order to control the amount of blood passing through them. This is known as the peripheral resistance. Once through the arterioles the blood percolates through the tiny *capillaries* where it then gives up its oxygen and food to the body's cells and in turn receives their waste products and carbon dioxide.

The blood then passes through the *venules* (smaller veins) which join to form the larger *veins*, which then return the blood to the heart and lungs for recirculation. Most of the force imparted by the heart's contraction has been used up by the time the blood reaches the veins. These veins, therefore, have to overcome the force of gravity (except those located in the upper 1/3 of the body) in order to return the blood to the heart.

The return of blood to the heart by way of these veins is dependent on many factors, one of the most important being the presence of uni-directional (one-way) *valves* located along the walls of the veins, which prevent the backflow of blood. These valves are aided by the contractions of the muscles in the legs (sometimes referred to as the *"muscle pump"*), which help to squeeze the leg veins and move the blood upwards back to the heart and lungs for re-circulation throughout the body.

Peripheral vascular disorders (diseases of the veins and arteries) are common problems in the aging population. A recent study showed that one out of every four elderly patients who visited the doctor complained of either pain, numbness, swelling or inflammation of one or both legs. We have seen how the blood is carried throughout the body by the three different types of blood vessels (arteries, capillaries and veins). The network formed by these three types of blood vessels constitute what is known as the *peripheral circulation*. Any diseases that affect any of these blood vessels are referred to as *peripheral vascular diseases*.

YOUR HEALTH'S SUPREME, WHEN YOUR ARTERIES ARE CLEAN

A 55-year-old male executive came to see me recently because of pain in his calf muscles when he walked. He was not able to walk more than a block before severe pain in one or both calves caused him to stop walking. After a few minutes of rest, the pain subsided and he could resume walking again. However, after walking another block or two at the most, the pain resumed and he was forced to sit down again. This patient had a history of moderate hypertension and he smoked 1½ packs of cigarettes every day since he was 20 years old. The diagnosis was relatively simple. The patient exhibited all of the classical symptoms of *"intermittent claudication."*

Intermittent claudication is defined as pain or cramps in the legs, usually the calf muscles, brought about by exercise (usually walking) and relieved fairly promptly by rest. This condition results from an occlusion (obstruction) in the large and medium-sized arteries leading to the legs. This obstruction comes from the build-up of deposits of cholesterol (atherosclerosis) inside of these blood vessels. As this obstruction becomes more severe, the blood supply to the exercising leg muscles cannot be met. Since these muscles cannot get enough oxygen, they cry out with pain (intermittent claudication) due to the lack of oxygen-rich blood. When the exercise (walking) is stopped, the muscles require less oxygen, so that as soon as the limited blood supply reaches these muscles with some oxygen, the pain stops.

The very first step in the treatment of this condition is to stop smoking. Carbon monoxide from smoking promotes atherosclerosis in both the coronary arteries and in the peripheral arteries (those leading away from the heart—example: legs). Carbon monoxide molecules actually jump into the seats on the red blood cells that were reserved for the oxygen molecules. Without its passenger, oxygen, the red blood cell carries this deadly enemy (carbon monoxide) throughout the body. These carbon monoxide molecules get off at various stops along the arteries to do their dirty work. The arteries waiting for oxygen get a big surprise. They get molecules of carbon monoxide instead. This carbon monoxide irritates the artery's inner lining (intima) and subsequently makes it an ideal seeding bed for deposits of cholesterol.

Nicotine from the cigarettes also contributes to piling up more cholesterol in the arteries. It accomplishes this by raising the blood pressure, narrowing down the artery's opening (lumen) and by promoting clot formation in the arteries. When you stop smoking you can prevent atherosclerosis from progressing and in some cases you can actually reverse the process.

The simplest and often most effective treatment for this condition is—yes, you guessed it—*walking!* Now wait a minute, you're thinking, "he just told me that walking is what caused the pain in intermittent claudication." That's absolutely correct. However, most medical authorities feel that a gradual walking program is the best form of conservative therapy for this condition. Patients who have stopped smoking and engaged in a modified walking program have been able to double or triple the distance that they can walk without pain. This occurs because walking dilates or opens the arteries, making more room available for blood to reach the muscles. Walking also makes more oxygen available to be carried in its regular seat on the red blood cell. This extra oxygen prevents cholesterol from being deposited in the arteries and it supplies more nourishment to these oxygen-starved muscles. And walking helps to keep the arteries elastic, so that they can stretch and recoil, thus helping to propel the blood along its way.

Finally, walking improves the flow of blood to these muscles by opening up a reserve group of blood vessels, that normally just sit in the wings like under-studies in a play. These reserve blood vessels are re-ferred to as the *collateral circulation*. Walking actually calls forth these small little-used reserve blood vessels, much the same as the trumpeter calls forth the caval-ry. These small vessels located in the legs open up with regular walking and send the blood around (bypass) the blocked arteries. A regular walking program can help to keep these collateral vessels open permanently.

Walking also can actually eat away at the choles-terol deposits that have accumulated in the blocked arteries. It accomplishes this by supplying oxygen-rich blood to these blocked arteries and by raising the good (HDL cholesterol) which carries shovelfuls of these cholesterol deposits out of the body. Walking also low-ers the bad (LDL cholesterol) in the blood, making less cholesterol available to block-up the arteries.

If, however, this disease has progressed too far, then medical treatment may be required. Several new drugs that help to open the arteries and decrease the blood's thickness (viscosity) are now available. If these medications are not effective, then surgery may be necessary. One form of surgery is called *angioplasty*, wherein the artery is dilated with a balloon catheter. The cholesterol plaque is actually squashed against the wall of the artery, making a larger opening available for the passage of blood. The other form of surgery is called *arterial bypass surgery*. In this type of surgery, a vein graft is usually attached to the artery above and below the blockage, so that blood actually bypasses the blocked artery. Often times an attempt is also made to remove the blockage inside the artery (*endarterectomy*). These procedures, especially the bypass surgery, are risky and are only done in those cases where no other treatment is successful.

There is a similar type of condition in which cholesterol deposits accumulate in the arteries of the neck (carotid arteries). This form of atherosclerosis obstructs the flow of blood through these arteries and results in a decrease in the supply of oxygen-rich blood to the cells of the brain. This decreased blood supply can lead to a condition referred to as *transient ischemic attacks* (TIA's). These are actually temporary small strokes with no permanent damage. These attacks can cause visual loss, speech impairment, weakness or partial paralysis of an arm or leg, memory loss, headaches and other neurological symptoms. These symptoms usually last a few seconds to several minutes and then the patient is normal again. Some cases have been known to last several hours. If this process of atherosclerosis progresses to a point where the carotid arteries are almost completely blocked, then vascular surgery may be necessary to prevent a full-blown stroke from occurring.

The best treatment for both of these conditions is to prevent them from occurring. Always check with your physician if you develop any symptoms that you think might be caused by these disorders. The risk factors for developing these diseases are the same as the risk factors for developing heart disease. Cigarette smoking, high serum cholesterol, inactivity, stress, excess caffeine and alcohol, obesity, diabetes and hypertension can all be modified or corrected by walking. Remember, walking keeps your *arteries clean* and your *health supreme*. Keep claudication pain and transient ischemia away, with a *walk each day*.

VEINS' VITAL VALVES: VANDALIZED VICTIMS

Once your blood has circulated throughout the arteries, supplying oxygen and nutrients to all of your body's cells, it must return to the heart and lungs for a fresh supply of oxygen. The blood must pass from the arteries into the veins before it can be returned to the heart and lungs. Except for the blood returning to the heart from the upper third of the body, the return of all the rest of the blood to the heart from the lower two-thirds of the body must go upwards against the force of gravity.

This flow of blood through the veins back to the heart is assisted by the contraction of your *leg muscles* when you walk. The leg muscles actually squeeze the blood up the veins against gravity. This upward flow of blood is also aided by the small *one-way valves* located inside the walls of the veins. These valves actually prevent the blood from falling back down the veins.

Prolonged sitting actually causes a pooling of blood in the leg veins because of the force of gravity. This results in a build-up of pressure inside the walls of the veins and subsequently impairs the return flow of blood back to the heart. I'm sure you've experienced *numbness* and *tingling* in your legs when you've been sitting in one position for a long time. Once you get up and walk around, your leg muscles begin to squeeze the pooled blood back up the leg veins, and the symptom of numbness quickly goes away.

Some people unfortunately have genetically weak veins. These individuals are prone to develop varicose veins. Prolonged sitting, as we have seen, builds up the venous pressure in the leg veins which is caused by the pooling of blood. Anyone who has weak veins to start with, now faces a more serious problem than just numbness and tingling in the legs. The excessive pressure that builds up in the veins actually balloons out these weak veins. This, in turn, stretches out the walls of the veins, and the small valves located inside the walls of the veins lose their resiliency.

After a period of time these weakened veins permanently dilate (enlarge), and their valves no longer are able to prevent the flow of blood from dropping back down the veins. This results in what is commonly called *varicose* or *incompetent veins,* which are unable to return all of the blood back to the heart. Sometimes fluid leaks out of these veins into the tissues of the legs causing edema (swelling of the feet and legs). Walking and support stockings are the only ways to control this condition. Surgery sometimes is necessary if these veins become worse.

Prolonged sitting can result in another more serious, often life-threatening, condition of the veins. The blood that pools in the leg veins of those people who sit in one position for long periods of time may begin to clot. This stagnated blood starts to irritate and inflame the inside walls of the veins it is pressing against. This inflammation of the leg veins is called *phlebitis.* This condition requires prompt medical treatment and can be a potentially life-threatening condition. If a blood clot actually forms in these veins it could conceivably become dislodged and travel to the heart or lungs with fatal consequences. Although this condition occurs more frequently in people with varicose veins, it can occur in anyone who sits in one position for a long period of time (example: long flights or auto trips).

After you have been sitting for a long time, especially when traveling, your circulation slows down. This is why your feet often swell after a long trip. The upward flow of blood from the leg veins can also be impaired by constrictive clothing or by crossing your legs, which causes further swelling in your feet and ankles. Always make it a point to walk around on a plane or train. Make frequent stops when riding in a car to stretch your legs. Walking will start your leg muscle pump working, so that it squeezes the blood up your leg veins and back into your heart for re-circulation. Don't let your leg *veins' vital valves* become *vandalized victims* of the *sedentary burglar.*

A PHILADELPHIA PHENOMENON

Harry Broadbent, a 92-year-old resident of Philadelphia, was in danger of losing a leg ten years ago because of poor circulation. Harry was unable to take medication because of the side effects and was facing possible surgical amputation of his leg.

Harry decided to begin a walking program, under his doctor's supervision. According to Harry, "I mean walk, like I was really going somewhere." Harry decided to become an all purpose messenger for the various business establishments in the Northeast Philadelphia area.

On a typical day Harry walks about 4 to 5 miles, starting at 9:00 AM in the morning, and does various and sundry messenger tasks. For instance, he picks up mail at the various business establishments and posts it at one of the Northeast Philadelphia post offices, takes orders for stamps, carries shoes to repair shops and any other general errands. Harry does not take pay for this messenger service and is happy to state that after 10 years as a messenger his circulation has improved and his legs still carry him his 4 to 5 miles daily and he may, in fact, be the world's oldest walking messenger.

LOOK 10 TO 15 YEARS YOUNGER!

How would you like to look 10, 15, maybe 20 years younger than you look right now? It's as easy as one, two, three. One—avoid too much sun. Two—don't smoke. Three—walk every day. Sound simple? It is! And it works!

The more you expose yourself to the **sun**, the more your skin wrinkles permanently. A summer tan lasts forever in the form of wrinkles because the connective tissue (supporting structures) under the skin buckles, pulling down the skin overlying the area. No amount of face creams or lotions will ever be able to correct the problem. And don't forget the high incidence of skin cancer caused by overexposure to the sun. The sun may be fun, but don't get too well-done. Always use blocking lotions to protect your skin from wrinkles and skin cancer.

A study of over 500 face-lift patients found that the surgical skin flap dies and falls off more often in smokers than non-smokers. Also, it was noted that the skin wounds in smokers heal more slowly and were more prone to infection than those in non-smokers. The reason: **cigarette smoke decreases the blood supply to the skin** which leads to poor healing.

Why suffer the slings and arrows of the surgeon's knife to lift-up your face, when a few puffs of your cigarette will make it droop again? I can always tell a cigarette smoker, who incidentally always looks older than their age, by the wrinkles in his or her face, even if I've never seen the patient before. This is especially true of a woman's skin which appears to be more severely affected by the ravages of smoking. It starts to wrinkle as early as age 30.

Walking is nature's own face-lift. Each time you take a brisk walk the oxygen-rich blood supply travels to all the tiny pores in your face giving it a natural pink glow. Walking increases the blood supply to the skin all over the body, providing it with oxygen and nutrients to keep the skin and its underlying supportive structures healthy and firm. Take a good look at your senior citizen friends and relatives and I'll bet that you'll be able to tell who the walkers are. Provided that they're not smokers, their skin will appear healthy and pink, not pasty, and almost wrinkle free.

WALKING WOMEN—UNITE!

Osteoporosis is a serious debilitating disease, affecting over 20 million Americans, mostly women over the age of 45. This condition is actually a degeneration of bone throughout the body resulting in a loss of bone density. The bones actually become thinned out as a result of a loss of the mineral calcium from the bone structure. Osteoporosis is especially marked after menopause because of a reduction in the secretion of estrogen by the aging ovaries.

Osteoporosis leads to approximately 1½ million fractures each year. Fractures of the hips are particularly common in older women. Approximately one out of five older women who sustains a hip fracture dies of secondary complications. This results in almost 35,000 deaths every year, making osteoporosis a leading cause of death among senior citizens. Another 25% of these women who break their hips become permanently crippled. Other serious complications of osteoporosis are fractures of the spinal column. These fractures can cause a collapse of the spinal vertebrae resulting in a shortening of actual height, a severe curvature of the spine ("dowager's hump,"), or a paralysis of the spinal cord.

There are many therapies that are currently undergoing investigation for the treatment of osteoporosis. The most common form of treatment is the use of calcium supplements to replace the calcium lost from bone. Other recommended treatments include the use of estrogen, sodium flouride, vitamin D supplements and calcitrol (a form of vitamin D that helps the absorption of calcium). Enough about treatment. What do you think is the most important way to prevent osteoporosis? You guessed it again! **Walking!**

In a recent study reported in The Journal of Orthopedic Research women who remained physically active after menopause or after age 50 had stronger, denser bones. Compared with inactive women ages 50-75, the active women had considerably greater arm and spine bone density measurements, almost in the same range as women 10-15 years younger. This study supports earlier research that shows that **osteoporosis** (thinning of the bones) can be slowed or halted by a regular walking program combined with a high calcium diet, and that the incidence of bone fractures is 10 times less frequent in "**walking women.**"

Walking outdoors when the sun is shining also helps to strengthen bones, because sunshine helps the body produce vitamin D, a nutrient needed for calcium absorption. And if these walking women ever do have the misfortune to break a bone—their bones **unite** (heal) faster!

BEAT THE CLOCK

At the cell's molecular level we find that exercise keeps your body's cells infused with adequate amounts of oxygen. After the age of 25, inactivity reduces the cellular activity of our body's tissues 1 percent per year, as the amount of oxygen distributed through the cells of our body slowly starts to decrease.

Moderate exercise, on the other hand, improves the efficiency of the heart and lungs to supply increased amounts of oxygen throughout the body. In a recent study, unconditioned males and females ages 60 to 83 showed improved breathing capacity by 29 percent in one year after a moderate walking program. In another study, middle-aged men 40 to 60 who engaged in a walking program had cardiovascular systems twice as capable as sedentary men of the same age group.

Strenuous exercise also has been shown to improve the efficiency of the heart and lungs to supply increased oxygen to the individual cells; however, since the activity of the exercising and respiratory muscles has increased significantly during strenuous exercise, most of this extra oxygen is needed for respiration and muscular activity. The remainder (what oxygen is left over), therefore, is supplied to the rest of the cells of the body. As we have previously seen, this shunting of blood away from the non-exercising parts of the body may have hazardous effects.

All the major studies on longevity and exercise to date have been based on moderate exercises like walking. These medical reports compared moderately active people versus sedentary people, not fitness nuts versus sedentary individuals. No one has ever proved that joggers live longer than walkers or sedentary people. In fact, most joggers don't live long enough to get included in the studies.

WALK DON'T DIE: HERE ARE THE REASONS WHY

1. **Walking lowers the blood pressure by**:
   a. **dilating (opening) the arteries**, allowing more blood to flow through them
   b. improving **elasticity** of blood vessels—giving less resistance to the flow of blood
   c. lowering chemicals in blood that can raise blood pressure —**catecholamines** and **angiotensin**

    d. improving **return of blood** to the heart, so that the heart can work more efficiently at a slower rate

    e. increasing the amount of **oxygen** delivered to all tissues and cells

    f. decreasing the rate of **sodium reabsorption** in the kidneys

2. **Walking protects the heart by**:
   a. decreasing the risk of **blood clot** formation
   b. improving the return of blood to the heart from the **leg veins**
   c. increasing the flow of blood through the **coronary arteries**
   d. increasing **HDL (good) cholesterol** which protects the heart and arteries against fatty deposits (plaque)
   e. improving the efficiency of the heart's **cardiac output** (total volume of blood pumped out by the heart each minute)
   f. helping to keep the **collateral circulation** open and available for emergencies

3. **Walking improves lung efficiency and breathing capacity by**:
   a. conditioning the **muscles of respiration** (chest wall and diaphragm)
   b. opening more **usable lung space** (alveoli)
   c. improving efficiency of **extracting oxygen** from the air

4. **Walking improves the general circulation by**:
   a. increasing the **total volume of blood**, and the amount of red **blood cells**, allowing more oxygen to be carried in the bloodstream
   b. **dilating the arteries** thus improving blood flow
   c. increasing **flexibility of arteries** thus lowering blood pressure
   d. compression of **leg and abdominal veins** by the

pumping action of the muscles used in **walking**, aiding the return of blood to the heart

e. using small blood vessels in the legs for re-routing blood (**collateral circulation**) around blocked arteries in emergencies

5. **Walking prevents the build-up of fatty deposits (plaque) in arteries by**:
   a. decreasing the serum **triglycerides** (sugar fats)
   b. decreasing **LDL (bad) cholesterol** in the blood
   c. increasing **HDL (good) cholesterol** in the blood
   d. preventing the blood from getting too thick, thus lessening the chance that **blood clots** will form

6. **Walking promotes weight loss and weight control by**:
   a. directly **burning calories**
   b. regulating the brain center (**appestat**) to control appetite
   c. re-directing **blood flow** away from digestive tract toward the exercising muscles thus decreasing appetite
   d. using **blood fats** instead of sugar as a source of energy

7. **Walking controls stress by**:
   a. increasing relaxation hormones in the brain (**Beta-endorphins**) and decreasing stress hormones (**epinephrine** and **norepinephrine**)
   b. increasing the **oxygen** supply and decreasing the amount of **carbon dioxide** to the brain
   c. efficient utilization of **blood sugar** in the body regulated by an improved production of **insulin**
   d. literally **walking away** from stress

8. **Walking promotes a longer healthier life by**:
   a. strengthening the **heart muscle** and regulating the **cardiac output** (a slower more efficient heart rate)

b. lowering **blood pressure** thus preventing strokes, heart attacks and kidney disorders
c. improving **lungs' efficiency** in extracting oxygen from the air
d. improving the efficiency of the delivery of **oxygen** to all the body's organs, tissues and cells
e. strengthening **muscle fibers** throughout the body thus improving reaction time and maintaining muscle tone
f. maintaining **bone strength and structure** by preserving the mineral content of the bone preventing osteoporosis (bone thinning) and certain forms of arthritis

WALK ON AND ON AND ON AND ON————

Harry Truman once told reporters, "I believe walking will make me live longer." Truman lived to be 88. Until the age of 90 Rose Kennedy walked 3-4 miles every day. The famous singer Hildegarde used to say "I get out and walk every day, rain or shine, blizzard or flood. I have to do it. I have to get that action—the legs, the arms, the bloodstream."

Dr. Alexander Leaf, former Chief of Medicine at Massachusetts General Hospital and now the Chairman of the Department of Preventive Medicine and Clinical Epidemiology at Harvard Medical School, studied people all over the world who had lived long lives and he concluded from his research that—"It is apparent that an exercise like walking throughout life is an important factor promoting well-being and longevity. One is never too old to commence a regular program of exercise and once started, will never grow too old to continue it."

At a world wide medical convention on Aging & Exercise held at the National Institutes of Health in Bethesda, MD it was concluded that walking is the most efficient and safest form of exercise for people of all ages. It was also concluded that regular walking was the only safe way to a long healthy life.

There no longer is any doubt that walking will prolong your life. Research has given us the answers why, it's better to **WALK THAN DIE!**

13 STEPS TO PREVENT YOUR DEATH

1. Get a complete physical exam by your family physician at least once a year. Follow through on any tests that he suggests.
2. Take any medication prescribed by your physician on a regular basis, unless otherwise specified. For example, some medications can be stopped after a week or two, others may have to be continued indefinitely.
3. Report any unusual signs or symptoms to your doctor immediately. For example, chronic cough, change in bowel habits, any lumps or masses, bleeding of any kind, weight loss, loss of appetite, headaches, dizziness, fatigue, chest pain, shortness of breath, cuts that won't heal, respiratory, intestinal, urinary or gynecological symptoms, or pain or discomfort anywhere in your body.
4. Follow up regularly with your physician for any condition that he may be treating you for. Many disorders don't go away just because you've finished the bottle of pills (example: high blood pressure).
5. Follow the **24** good **S's** and avoid the **24** bad **S's** in Chapter 4.
6. Eat all of the fabulous, fantastic foods for good health that start with an **F** in Chapter 7.
7. Stop smoking and decrease alcohol and caffeine intake.

8. Eat less salt, sugar, saturated fat and cholesterol. Eat more fiber.
9. Keep your weight down. Change your philosophy from, "I live to eat," to "I just eat to live" (Chapter 9—**DIETSTEP**®).
10. Learn to deal with stress and tension sensibly. Allow enough time every day for rest and relaxation.
11. Do the **HEARTSTEP** (Chapter 13) to live longer without bypass surgery.
12. Keep your feet on the ground and your blood pressure down with the **STRESS-STEP** (Chapter 14).
13. Don't let life pass you by, **WALK, DON'T DIE.**

"I WISH SOME OF MY FRIENDS OVER THERE HAD READ THIS BOOK!"

"TAKE YOUR CREW BACK TO THE HOSPITAL, YOUNG FELLOW.
I'VE OUTWALKED MY LAST THREE DOCTORS!"

INDEX